Zalmoxis

by   Doris C. Plantus

Zalmoxis

Fifth Estate Publishing, Blountsville, AL 35031

Cover Designed by Nancy Karen Ferrel

Printed on acid-free paper

Library of Congress Control No: 2020953011

ISBN: 9781936533886

Fifth Estate, 2020

Zalmoxis

Doris C. Plantus

Table of Contents

Zalmoxis

For Maria, Raveca, Ana, and Iosif

Preface

Lucian Blaga, who is judged by many to be Romania's most original philosopher and one of her greatest poets of the twentieth century, is relatively little known in Western Europe and the English-speaking world. The reasons are not hard to find: he wrote in a language whose range was limited practically to a single country, and he represented a culture whose integration into Western European philosophical and literary currents was of comparatively recent origin. But in his own country he was a key figure in the intellectual and cultural life of the interwar period: he created a sublime poetry and constructed an intriguing philosophy of mystery; he made bold experiments in the drama; and he immersed himself in the great debate about Romanian national identity and paths of development. His accomplishments in each of these fields were exceptional, but his work, nonetheless, forms a whole. We cannot divide his philosophy, poetry, and drama into separate compartments, for the same metaphysical strivings and acute sensibility pervade all three.

I

Blaga was born on May 9, 1895 in the village of Lancrăm in southern Transylvania, where his father was the Orthodox parish priest. Impressions of childhood spent in the village, a time of wonder and discovery by his own account, left powerful residues in his lyricism and his philosophy of culture. Although he left the village for the city to continue his education, he never ceased to draw inspiration from it as from an inexhaustible source of myth and metaphor. He was attracted early to philosophy. His wide, but undirected readings while attending the Orthodox gymnasium in Braşov and the Orthodox Theological-Pedagogical Institute in Sibiu achieved sharper focus at the University of Vienna, where he studied during the latter years of the First World War. This sojourn in Vienna and shorter visits after the war deepened his attachment to certain currents of German philosophy, which he found congenial to his own probing of the nature of existence and man's place in the cosmos. His experience of intellectual life in Vienna reinforced his enormous admiration for Goethe and Nietzsche and confirmed his adherence to the "new style," or Expressionism, in literature, as his first columns of poetry clearly reveal.

The union of Transylvania, which had been a part of the Austro-Hungarian Monarchy, with Romania at the end of the First World War brought a new orientation in Blaga's intellectual life. In a sense, he was drawn away from Vienna to Bucharest, the cultural center as well as the political capital of Greater Romania. His creativity inevitably took new directions as he contributed unreservedly to the intellectual effervescence of interwar Romania. Yet, despite his enthusiasm, he could not but share with many of his colleagues the sense of spiritual unease that pervaded Romania and Europe as a whole. Like intellectuals elsewhere, he was disillusioned with positivism and science and felt overwhelmed by the inability of reason to explain the deeper meaning of life and offer solace for humankind's perilous temporal journey and assurances about the hereafter. As he searched for permanent spiritual values he relied on an intuitive approach and an exploration of the irrational and the unconscious, although he never denied to reason and will and important role in his quest.

The interwar years were a time of intensive creativity fir Blaga, a time when he produced the body of work that secured his place in Romanian letters. There were seven volumes of poetry, from *Poemele luminii* (*The Poems of Light*) in 1919 to *Nebănuitele trepte* (*Unsupected Steps*) in 1943. In philosophy he began the construction of his system in the 1920s with "stages" such as his doctoral dissertation, *Cultura și cunoștința* (*Culture and Knowledge*), which he defended at the University of Vienna in 1920. They were followed by the nine "building blocks" of the 19302 that formed the monumental trilogies: *Trilogia cunoașterii* (*The Trilogy of Knowledge*) in 1943, *Trilogia culturii* (*The Trilogy of Culture*) in 1944, and *Trilogia valorilor* (*The Trilogy of Values*) in 1946. He also experimented with the drama, and his ten plays, from *Zamolxe* in 1921 to *Arca lui Noe* (*Noah's Ark*) in 1944, ran the gamut from seemingly "folkloric" plats to Freudian dramas and to plays that sought to define the national character and understand man's creative vocation.

In the interwar period Blaga remained aloof from political struggle and did not become active on behalf of any major social cause. But he was by no means indifferent to the world around him. He produced a constant stream of articles for newspapers and periodicals, usually on cultural questions and with special reference to current and controversial issues. He also entered public service. In 1926 he accepted an appointment as press attaché at the Romanian legation in Warsaw, thus beginning a career in diplomacy that took him to similar posts in Prague, Belgrade, Bern, and Vienna, and culminated in his being named minister to Portugal in April 1938, a position he held until the following spring. Public honors also came to him. He was elected a member of the Romanian Academy in 1936, and in 1938, he was appointed to the chair of the philosophy of culture at the University of Cluj, a position created especially for him. For the next decade he used this unique forum to mold a new generation of intellectuals.

The normal course of academic life in Cluj and Blaga's own creative preoccupations were interrupted by the cession of northern Transylvania to Hungary in August 1940, a loss of territory and population forced upon Romania by Germany and Italy. Blaga was soon able to resume his work in Sibiu, where the University of Cluj had taken refuge. Besides teaching and writing, he founded and edited *Saeculum*, a review devoted to problems of philosophy, where he published essays of his own that were to form parts of new trilogies and welcomed the writings of others, even critics of his philosophical ideas. He also participated in a literary circle of gifted young writers and critics who, like him, were intent on giving Romanian literature a modern aesthetic and philosophical grounding. He returned to Cluj in 1945, following the expulsion of German and Hungarian armies from northern Transylvania.

Blaga was caught up in great political and social ferment in the immediate postwar years, as the Romanian Communist Party, supported by the Soviet Union, whose troops occupied the country, gradually imposed a one-party dictatorship based on the Soviet model. In the educational and cultural institutions of the new regime there was no room for men like Blaga. In 1948 he was removed from the University of Cluj and the Romanian Academy and, in effect, reduced to silence. Although he continued to write poetry and elaborate his philosophical system, neither of these activities was congenial to the new order and were works, as he put it himself, intended for the desk drawer. Except for translations, notably Goethe's *Faust* in 1955 and Lessing's *Nathan the Wise* in 1956, he published little of his own work until the last year of his life, when a few poems and short newspaper articles appeared. He died on May 6, 1961 in Cluj from cancer.

In the early 1960s a reevaluation of Blaga's creativity got under way. As the Communist Party placed increasing emphasis on the national culture, new editions of his poetry and, later, his philosophical works were published, and literary critics and historians undertook searching investigations of his work and life. The fall of the Communist regime in 1989 removed the remaining ideological constraints on the treatment of his philosophical and aesthetic ideas and led to comprehensive critical assessments of his place in Romania letters.

II

Blaga occupies a singular place in the history of Romanian philosophy. Because of the problems and the methods that preoccupied him, he stood apart from his Romanian contemporaries. Engrossed in his own original pursuit of the absolute, he undertook to elucidate the nature of being and to discover the meaning of existence in ways other than those belonging to the philosophical tradition of his own country. He was, rather, indebted to European sources, and he regarded himself as belonging to a tradition of European thought that had its origins in Classical Greece. Blaga shared the leading ideas of that great turn in European thought that occurred in the 1890s. Like Freud, Bergson, and others, who were its harbingers, and however much he might differ from them in detail, he accepted their general proposition that the ultimate foundation of human activity lay elsewhere than in logical thinking and that knowledge isolated from non-logical influences was impossible. Yet, like them, he could not dispense with reason and used the accepted methods of rational argument in explaining his own theories of cosmic and human development. Even so, he was forever dissatisfied with the explanations of man's condition set forth by nineteenth-century rationalism.

Foremost among the sources from which he drew in constructing his own system was German philosophy. His debt to Goethe, the German Romantics, and Nietzsche was immense, and he readily acknowledged it. He warmly praised Goethe as one of the few philosophers of the time to take his experiments in the natural sciences seriously. He was impressed especially by Goethe's ability to contemplate natural phenomena from a perspective of spatial and temporal wholeness, and he, too, sought the *Urphänomen,* or primordial phenomenon, which elucidated the nature of entire cultures and civilizations. He may also have owed to Goethe his aversion to the sort of rationalistic analysis, which, he thought, rather than illuminating its objects, pulverized it. As for the German Romantics, they turned his thought to myth and metaphysics and led him into those vague, secluded regions where his creative imagination could soar. They taught him that neither philosophy nor poetry was possible without magic thought, and later, as his own philosophical system matured, he confessed that in metaphysics thought ceased to be philosophy at all and, instead, became "mythosophy." He returned again and again to the works of Friederich Schelling as he sought to explain the nature of cultures and civilizations, and his first published essay in 1914 attempted to link Schelling's intellectual intuition with Goethe's method of the *Urphänomen*.

From Nietzsche he learned to appreciate cultural style and to question established spiritual values. Nietzsche's challenge to the world as it was, with its mechanized and urbanized civilization, calmed Blaga's spiritual anguish. He found comfort in Nietzsche's vitalism and doctrine of the will, which counteracted the "intellectualism" that stifled modern man's exuberance and dulled his creative flow. Like Nietzsche, he aspired to the absolute. Thus, it is impossible to study Blaga's writings on the philosophy of culture without being struck by the similarity to Nietzsche's mode of thought or to read Blaga's play *Zamolxe* without feeling the presence of Zarathustra.

Blaga drew many of his ideas about the comparative study of cultures and civilizations from Oswald Spengler. The "morphological method" that Spengler applied to the study of human history in *The Decline of the West*, published in two volumes in 1918 and 1922, greatly affected his own theory of style. Although they disagreed on many crucial points, Blaga's preference for "feeling" and "intuition" instead of "dissection analysis" found a justification in Spengler's work. He also shared Spengler's theory that the West, confounded by mechanization and standardization, had reached the end of its evolutionary cycle and was now ripe for the coming of a new spiritual age, a "new primitivism" in which men could regain their fascination for mystery and the supernatural.

At the heart of Blaga's philosophy was his eagerness to grasp the meaning of existence and to discover man's role in the universe. In his quest he confronted directly the great enigmas that obscured man's destiny, and he accepted the unknown for what it was: a mystery that could never be fully revealed. Indeed, mystery was fundamental to his philosophy in the same way that the "idea" was for Plato or the "category" for Kant. Blaga's world was saturated with mysteries of all kinds, and he lamented that philosopher had neglected or shunned altogether the idea of mystery. For him mystery was not the completely unknowable but an obscurity not yet adequately illuminated. It was full of meaning precisely because it concealed so much, and this overpowering incitement to investigation led Blaga into the depths of the human psyche and into the farthest limits of human reason.

As for man's place in the cosmos, Blaga showed no hesitation in assigning him to the horizon of mystery. In the trilogies he insisted that man's vocation could be none other than to reveal mystery and that, in so doing, he became the creator of culture. All these things, Blaga argued, had been determined ontologically: man was a creator of culture simply because he was man, because he belonged to a mode of existence that was exclusively human.

Blaga judged his own role as philosopher from this perspective. As a metaphysician he took it as his duty to create a world of his own and confessed that if he failed to do so, he would consider his vocation unfulfilled. He was thus intent upon penetrating the mystery of existence, but he harbored no illusions about the truth that such an endeavor might bring forth. He was certain that the attainment of ultimate truth was beyond man's capability because of the limitations on his knowledge of the absolute were inherent in his very mode of existence. Truth, then, in the usual meaning of the term, could not,

Blaga concluded in *Trilogia cunoașterii*, be the object of the creative act. Instead, he proposed attainable goals such as "the possible," "the imaginable," and "the beautiful." Even so, he recognized the supreme dignity of the human spirit in striving to know the unknowable, and he insisted that it took the place of divine revelation in exposing, in however fragmentary a fashion, the nature of being.

Blaga was intrigued by how man approached the unknowable, that is, by what mechanisms he created culture, and thus he was led to investigate cultural style. By the term style he did not mean the outward form of a work of art or literature but rather its manner of being. It was style, he argued in *Trilogia culturii*, that imbued works of art and literature and even entire ethnic communities and historical periods with their unique character; it was style that revealed the hidden side of human nature and thus became the principal means of revealing human spirituality; and it was style that caused creativity to differ from individual to individual, people to people, and period to period.

Besides mystery, the unconscious was an indispensable component of Blaga's theory of style. Indeed, he located this source of style in the unconscious, and, thus, his theory of style and his entire philosophy of culture were based on the proposition that creative acts, such as the structuring of a work or art, a philosophical theory, or a scientific hypothesis were directed by powers beyond the control of the conscious. As he put it, style was the "supreme yoke" which held an author, a current, or an entire culture in bondage and from which none could escape. Although he did not question the important contribution that the conscious made to the external elaboration of style, he denied that man's fundamental way of being, his "inner style" could be substantially altered by his own will.

Blaga took issue with those who dismissed the unconscious as a zone of primitive, animal impulses devoid of creativity or as a kind of basement of the conscious to which a multitude of suppressed or unwanted emotions had been consigned. On the contrary, he argued, the unconscious was a psychic reality possessing its own "sovereign" functions and an internal order and equilibrium of unlimited creative virtues. He admired Jung especially for having enriched the doctrine of the unconscious through his theory of psychic archetypes, which Blaga adapted for his own conception of the unconscious categories, and through his theory of the collective unconscious, which helped Blaga to account for the continuity of cultural style through the centuries.

Blaga endowed the unconscious with a series of categories, which, structurally, resembled Kant's categories of the conscious. They were the determinants of style and, grouped together, they formed a general pattern, or "stylistic matrix," which imposed itself on every culture and endowed it with individuality. The primary and secondary categories of the matrix were capable of infinite combinations, which were thus responsible for the myriad variations of cultural style.

Blaga was fascinated not only by the theoretical aspects of style, but eagerly undertook to apply his ideas to Romanian culture, explaining its uniqueness by using the categories of the unconscious stylistic matrix. In his search for Romanian identity he made his most eloquent statement of his ideas in *Spaţiul mioritic*. By "mioritic space" he meant the *plai*, the ridge or slope of a hill usually covered with meadows, which appeared in Romanian folk ballads, notably the masterpiece *Miorița* (*The Little Ewe*). But for him the *plai* had other stylistic meanings: it was the spatial horizon specific to Romanian culture, the "infinitely undulating horizon" of hill and valley that formed the "spiritual substratum" of the anonymous creations of Romanian folk culture. From this unconscious horizon of the stylistic matrix Blaga derived the "massive" preference of Romanian folk poets for the alternation of accented and unaccented syllables and for the unique arrangement of peasant houses, which were separated by green spaces—the "unaccented syllables between the houses."

Blaga focused his attention on the rural world, where he thought the main constituent elements of Romanian spirituality lay. He conceived of the Romanian village as the locale of the organic, uniquely human mode of existence, the place where the generating sources of the native culture were the strongest and purest. In fact, when he spoke of "culture", he meant the creative life of the village, and it was through this culture, "our eternity revealed in time," that the Romanians participated in the great adventure of cosmic creation. He contrasted this culture, a product of the "rural soul," with "civilization," whose embodiment was the city, the creation of the mechanized, bourgeois world, whose collapse seemed to him close at hand. For him, the great urban center of the twentieth century was the locale of "non-creative" preoccupations such as the accumulation of positive knowledge and the formulation of rationalistic conceptions; it was the place where man lost his "cosmic sentiment" and his attachment ot the specifically human, organic mode of existence. But the village was for him always the preeminent zone of mythical thought, which assimilated concrete appearances and enabled man to enter into a creative relationship with existence.

III

Blaga's poetic craft evolved under the aegis of European modernism, especially of those poetic movements in the early decades of the century in Germany and Austria usually grouped together as Expressionism. He shared with the Expressionists and others the idea of poetry as an adventure in cognition, as an activity of the self-examining mind. Like them, he was continually reflecting upon the significance of the poetic act and translating his meditations into verse of profound metaphysical sensibility and beauty. Like them, too, he was distrustful of unbridled inspiration and personal exultation. Indeed, he thought of himself as a builder, as one who followed Apollo rather than Dionysus, who prized conscious creation, and whose occasional transports of enthusiasm never descended into chaos.

Of all the varied currents of creative ideas Blaga sampled in the early stages of his poetic career, German Expressionism was undoubtedly the most irresistible. He wrote about it with obvious enthusiasm, and it formed the basis of his theory and art of poetry in the 1920s. Expressionist aesthetics gave meaning and direction to his artistic aspirations and reinforced his longing to attain the absolute and his passionate search for the essence of life. He felt a close kinship with those Expressionists who were made desperate by a sense of isolation from ordinary humanity and, like them, he attributed the condition to an exaggerated intellectualism that numbed the ability to behave and feel normally. Together they found solace in Bergson's theory of the *élan vital*, which postulated an unceasing conflict between the inhibiting intellect and the unconscious flow of life, and they were anxious to return to some primordial form of existence when everything was feeling and stood in close communion with nature. Blaga also shared the spiritual despair of the Expressionists, who took literally Nietzsche's pronouncement that God was dead, and in his own poetry he strove to create an ideal world to answer the fundamental questions of existence.

Blaga's poetry and plays of the 1920s are among the most important manifestations of Expressionism in Romanian literature. The themes that predominate—the archetypal, the transcendental, and the apocalyptic—are essentially Expressionist. His sense of belonging to the European intellectual tradition, his German culture, his receptivity to the innovations of modernism, and his anxiety over the direction of the intellectual and spiritual life in contemporary Europe all explain his attraction to Expressionism. They gave substance and direction to his artistic and his intellectual aspirations.

The connection between Blaga's poetry and philosophy is evident, and Blaga himself insisted that his poetic expression could never be solely a spontaneous act of sensibility or inspiration, but had to be molded also by his metaphysical speculations. His preoccupation with philosophy is so manifest that no special effort to prove philosophical influences on his poetry is necessary. Yet, his poetry is not simply a more lyrical expression of his philosophy, and he himself denied that his poetry was merely one of ideas or was in some way didactic. Although a knowledge of his philosophical system is not required for appreciation of his poetry, nonetheless, a recognition of the great metaphors of his philosophy—the Great Anonymous One, luciferian cognition, and transcendental censorship—and an understanding of his theory of mystery enrich the spiritual background against which he projects his poetic visions.

The first poem of Blaga's first column of verse, *Poemele luminii*, laid the foundation of his vision of the world. The opening line, "I do not crush the world's corolla of wonder," expresses his intuition of cosmic life as being present in all things and his belief that all animate beings and inanimate objects share in the secret of eternity. In these postulates he discovers the meaning of human existence and recognizes his duty to pursue the unknown to its ultimate source. He expresses dissatisfaction with appearances and is persuaded that true reality exists in a magic substance which pervades the entire world of phenomena. This absolute essence, he insists, reveals itself to those who will be guided not by the mind, which destroys the secrets of things, but by "holy mystery," which enriches even the darkest horizons of existence.

Blaga''s cosmic vision does not admit of easy generalizations, but at the heart of it lies an essentially animist conception. Together with the idea of mystery it is fundamental to the nature of his poetry. In *Trilogia culturii*, he argued that every **aspect of reality**, every motion **from** the fluttering of a leaf to the falling of a ray of sunlight, participated in the joy and suffering of man. This inanimate world was nothing less than an extension of the human body: when the branch of a tree stirred man felt its swaying like a gesture of his arm, or he could fell light as a resurrection and colors as joyfulness.

Confronted by a world whose essences were the unknown and the impenetrable, Blaga pursued its infinite secrets undaunted. The reality he strove to understand was filled with contradictions that defied reason and logic. It became for him a religion not of the irrational but of the non-rational, where human intelligence could operate only at the intuitive level. This was the region he called "mystery." His poetic universe, as well as his philosophical system ultimately turn on this major metaphor. The same metaphysics of mystery, which pervades the trilogies, is mirrored in his volumes of poetry.. Yet, as we have seen, he did not write poems to illustrate his philosophy. Rather, he was responding to a deep lyrical calling;

Blaga's poetic approach to mystery took the form of mythic thinking. Indeed, he could not conceive of a poetry divorced from myth, for he believed it to be the only means of penetrating beyond mere logical appearances to the essence of things. Myth was a way of expressing intuited truths, of putting into words and images presentiments and ideas that could not be precisely formulated. He was convinced that certain realities could be dealt with more effectively through "mythic method," or "mythosophy," rather than by scientific, logical analysis.

Another of Blaga's devices for penetrating mystery was metaphor. He was certain that the hidden aspects of existence made themselves known through metaphor, which enabled Man to gain at least a glimpse of reality. The metaphor performed a function similar to that of mythic thinking by piercing those zones that were closed to reason. Both operated on the "edge of reason" where meaning could only be intuited and communicated obliquely. In Blaga's conception, therefore, metaphor and myth possessed crucial cognitive virtues through their ability to establish striking, original relations between things which in isolation would have little or no deeper significance.

Blaga combined restless philosophical inquiry with a delicate poetic sensibility to produce a unique body of work. In so doing, he made crucial contributions to Romanian poetry. He applied myth on a scale not seen before, and his boldness in using free verse in his early volumes helped to establish it as the dominant form of modern Romanian prosody.

IV

At about the time Blaga published his first volumes of poems and his first essays in the philosophy of culture he completed work on his first play, *Zamolxe*, his so-called "Dacian drama." Its appearance in 1921 was mainly a response to artistic and philosophical preoccupations that had already manifested themselves in two books of poetry, *Poemele luminii* in 1919 and *Paşii profetului* (The Footsteps of the Prophet) in 1921, and in *Cultura şi cunoştinţa*. Blaga turned to the drama, first of all, to satisfy his own creative aspirations. As a poet he was constantly testing new forms, and now he was eager to try his hand at the dramatic poem. He had already included several in *Paşii profetului*, and he intended *Zamolxe* to be his most ambitious experiment to date with the genre. As a philosopher he was eager to pursue his investigation of the mystery of existence and to deepen his understanding of cultural style. As we have seen, he was intrigued especially by the complexities of the Romanian cultural style and the apparent contradictions in its spiritual manifestations. He set forth his idea on the subject in an article, *"Revolta fondului nostru nelatin"* (The Revolt of our Non-Latin Sources), published in the same year as *Zamolxe.* In it he insisted that the Romanians were much more than Latins with their clarity, rationality, and classical sense of balance. He pointed ou that even though Latinity predominated, the Romanians also had a rich Slavic-Dacian heritage, exuberant and full of life, which from time to time forced its way into the Romanian consciousness. This revolt of their non-Latin sources, originating in the "metaphysical depths" of the Romanian spirit, violently disturbed its Latin symmetry and harmony and proved the infinite diversity of the Romanian cultural style. Blaga found himself powerfully drawn to the Dacians, one of the ancestors of the Romanians who had been conquered by the Romans at the beginning of the first century, A.D., because they appealed to his poetic sensibilities: he viewed their world as overflowing with vitality, open to nature, and yearning for the absolute.

Blaga chose Zamolxe as the hero of his play because he seemed to epitomize all that the Dacians represented spiritually. He was, to be sure, an historical figure. According to the ancient Greeks, Zalmoxis, as he was known, had been a Dacian slave to the philosopher Pythagoras on the island of Samos who had acquired great knowledge from his master and who had returned to the Dacians, bringing them the religious teachings he had assimilated. Among the Dacians he was a priest and prophet, and under the name Gebeleizis he was also a celestial deity. A cult developed around him, and temples were dedicated to his memory, one of which recalled the place to which he was said to have retired every three years to meditate.

In portraying his hero, Blaga drew on the information provided by ancient and modern historians, but *Zamolxe* is not an historical drama. Rather, Blaga was intent on exploring the most remote layers of Romanian spirituality, and he was guided by his philosophical inclinations and lyric sensibility. He put himself in the figure of Zamolxe, and thus the portrait of the Dacian prophet that emerges is, in some sense, a self-portrait. It is Blaga, disguised as Zamolxe, who confronts the mystery of existence and seeks the meaning of cultural style and who tests hypotheses that will reach their fullest expression later in the trilogies.

Zamolxe is divided into three acts of three scenes each, which introduce the principal characters—Zamolxe, the High Priest, and the Dacians—and depict their relations with one another. In composition the play resembles a poem, as Blaga reveals his characters through monologues and dialogues rather than through action. The main conflict is one of ideas between Zamolxe and the High Priest, who are at odds over how men shall relate to the world. The High Priest, who resides in the city, stands for the old order, the traditional polytheistic faith, which has become institutionalized and has separated the Dacians from nature. He represents the aspirations of established theology, which taught that the ultimate principle in the world was of a rational, intellectual nature. His god was Apollonic and, thus, from Blaga's perspective, he represented the Latin depths of the Romanian soul. But Zamolxe, who lives close to nature and shuns the city, heralds a new beginning, a religion that will reconcile the Dacians with their true essence. The Great Blind Man, whose truth he preaches, is an instinctual and vitalist divinity who instills in men a frenetic energy to experience life and to become emotionally fused with all of surrounding nature. He is a Dionysian divinity who symbolizes repressed unconscious impulses and is the spirit behind the intermittent revolts Blaga perceived of the Romanians' non-Latin essence. Blaga's attachment to Expressionist ideals is thus discernible in his treatment of the characters as vehicles of ideas and in his preference for primitive nature over the sophisticated metropolis.

The play opens with Zamolxe seated in front of a cave contemplating nature and feeling himself a part of nature and touching the mystery of existence. He had taken refuge there seven years earlier when the people had driven him from the city where he had preached a new religion, that of the Great Blind Man. At first, solitude had been congenial to him, but now he is ready to return to his people to share with them the wisdom he has acquired in seven years of meditation. Although he feels a duty to undertake this mission, he hesitates because it is contrary to his contemplative nature. As he thus stands between two worlds, one of reflection and the other of deeds, three visions appear to him one after the other: Socrates, Jesus, and Giordano Bruno. The message the bring him is an admonition to take action, but the fate they shared as prophets reinforces his presentiment of tragedy. Yet, in the end, he decides to leave the cave and return to the world of men. Zamolxe's mission to his people occurs at a time of spiritual crisis among the Dacians: the old gods are dead; men have ceased to honor them, and a reevaluation of all values is under way.

Despite his banishment, Zamolxe's teachings have steadily gained adherents among the people, and the old ecclesiastical order is threatened with dissolution as the people rebel and try to seize the temple and depose the High Priest. But the High Priest is resourceful. He spreads the word that Zamolxe is a god who descended among men to teach them youth and suffering. Calm immediately returns to the city and the populace asks the High Priest to place a statue of Zamolxe in the temple alongside the other gods. This he does only too gladly because he hopes to blunt Zamolxe's message by associating him with the old gods.

In the meantime, Zamolxe has arrived at a meadow outside the city. When he learns that he has been made a god, he hastens to the temple to challenge the High Priest, knowing that deification will transform him form a prophet of elemental vitality into a lifeless abstraction. Zamolxe throws down his statue, and the people, who do not recognize him, kill him with pieces of his own statue. Both Zamolxe and his teachings have seemingly perished, but the Dacian have a sudden revelation of the presence among them and in them of the Great Blind

Man, the revelation that Blaga refers to in the designation of his play as a "pagan mystery."

The central figure of the play is Zamolxe. It is he to whom all the other figures are connected, and it is he who, in essence, defines them. He is also the most complex, a contemplative and melancholy being who savors solitude, but who is also a reformer driven by a sense of mission to bring about a spiritual rebirth of his people. There are obvious similarities between Zamolxe and Christ, but they are superficial: Zamolxe was not a divinity, nor was his revelation divine. There are also similarities between Zamolxe and Nietzsche's superman, but Zamolxe is not Zarathustra. Even though Zamolxe's dispute with the High Priest, his attacks on the traditional gods, and his efforts to prepare men to accept new values are reminiscent of Zarathustra's diatribes against the priests and on al that was outmoded, Zamolxe was a gentler, more human figure who remained attached to the common people.

Through Zamolxe's sacrifice the Dacians rise above their immediate, primitive impulses, which were frenzied and wanton. As Zamolxe had taught them, the religion of the Great Blind Man symbolized the fusion of nature and the divine and was the embodiment of the creative, if sometimes aimless, power of nature. In embracing it, they cast aside the gods that the High Priest had set up between them and nature. They became themselves, that is, they returned to the deep unconscious sources of their faith, symbolized by a serene, mysterious communion with nature.

A Note on Further Reading:

On Lucian Blaga's life the fullest account is Ion Bălu, *Viaţa lui Lucian Blaga,* 4 vols. (Bucureşti, 1995-1999). George Gană offers a comprehensive, critical assessment of poetry and other literary work in *Opera literară a lui Lucian Blaga* (Bucureşti, 1976). The best critical edition of Blaga's poetry is
Opere, ed. George Gană, 6 vols. (Bucureşti, 1982-1997). Indispensible is D. Vatamaniuc, *Lucian Blaga, 1895-1961. Bibliografie* (Bucureşti, 1977).

The principal aspects of Blaga's philosophy are explained clearly and succinctly in Ovidiu Drimba, *Filosofia lui Blaga* Bucureşti, 1995), originally published in 1944. A many-sided examination of his theories of knowledge, values, and creativity is the collection of essays edited by Dumitru Ghişe, Angela Botez, and Victor Botez, *Lucian Blaga— Cunoaştere şi creaţie* (Bucureşti, 1987. One may also consult with profit Leonard Gavriliu, *Inconştientul în viziunea lui Lucian Blaga* (Bucureşti, 1997); Corin Braga, *Lucian Blaga. Geneza lumilor imaginare* (Iaşi, 1998); Andra Bruciu, *Lucian Blaga. Reflexe germane în filosofia culturii* (Bucureşti, 2006); and Traian Pop, *Lucian Blaga. Filosofia şi metafizica valorilor* (Cluj-Napoca, 2007). Indispensible is P. Diacono and M. Diaconu, *Dicţionar de termeni filosofici ai lui Lucian Blaga* (Bucureşti, 200).

Valuable introductions to Blaga the poet are Mariana Şora, *Cunoaştere poetică şi mit în opera lui Lucian Blaga* (Bucureşti, 1970); Milania Livada, *Iniţiere în poezia lui Lucian Blaga* (Bucureşti, 1974); Ion Pop, *Lucian Blaga. Universul liric* (Bucureşti,1981), and Eugen Todoran, *Lucian Blaga. Mit, poezie, mit poetic* (Bucureşti, 1997). On Blaga's poetic craft one may consult

with profit Ladislas Gáldi, *Contributions à l'histoire de la versification roumaine. La Prosodie de Lucian Blaga* (Budapest, 1972).

A useful general approach to Blaga the dramatist is Dan C. Mihăilescu, *Dramaturgia lui Lucian Blaga* (Cluj-Napoca, 1984). On specific aspects of his plays and playwriting one may consult Eugen Todoran, *Lucian Blaga. Mitul dramatic* (Timişoara, 1985) and Doina Modola, *Lucian Blaga şi teatrul Riscurile avangardei* (Bucureşti, 2003). Of great use is Constantin Cubleşan, ed., *Dicţionarul personajelor din teatrul lui Lucian Blaga* (Cluj-Napoca, 2005). The preceding works on

Zalmoxis

Blaga's plays contain critical appraisals of *Zamolxe*. To be consulted also is Braga's work mentioned above. The best critical edition of *Zamolxe* is in volume 3 of Ganǎ's edition of Blaga's *Opere*. His notes are indispensible.

Keith Hitchins

Translator's Foreword

My first translation of *Zamolxe, mister păgân,* emerged out of a translation seminar I took as a graduate student. While I remain proud of that first attempt, I realized some years ago, how much Blaga's play stood to gain by a fresh translation, all the more because I have made modest strides as a translator since then. This second edition, therefore, is a revised translation of my original version in which I have corrected previous errors—some large, some small, while reaffirming certain innovations I find as appropriate now, as they were intuitive back then.

The eloquence of Lucian Blaga's dramatic poem, *Zamolxe, mister păgân,* is its earnest attempt at fording an impossible barrier that separated a Latinized people from a dissociated non-Roman past. Recorded by Herodotus in his *Histories*, corroborated by Strabon and others, and perhaps more importantly, since sustained by oral tradition, Zalmoxis is reported to have been a prophet-priest to a branch of the Thracian people called Getae by Greek writers, and Dacian by the Romans. The Thracians were a ubiquitous tribe stretching from the north of Greece throughout the Balkans, with the Dacians occupying the Danube basin in present day Romania. Although Zalmoxis persists historically in an opaque light as an obscure, passionate hero in the orphic tradition, Blaga openly creates a myth that speaks to the complex and innovative religion of the Thracians at that time: the concept of immortality. He germinates the historical component of Zalmoxis into a mythical persona in order to explore the substance of the myth, thus the story of the enigmatic prophet-priest possesses little more than the invariant core conceived by ancient Dacians, in terms of factual content in Blaga's play. Herodotus, after all, identifies Zalmoxis as the god of the Dacian religion, whose central tenet was immortality. Beyond that, Zalmoxis is pure Blaga. That is to say, the man, and the myth are poeticized under the artistic and philosophical hand of one of Romania's most prominent poets and philosophers.

The dynamics of translating a work that in its own heart remains conflicted with issues of cultural transmission and autochthonomy presented curious challenges on several levels. Fortunately, Lucian Blaga is remarkable as a writer for his ability to reconcile poetical and philosophical arrays of reasonable inference. The latitude for convergent meaning is generous; the focus of Blaga's myth has a built-in inevitability that allows the task of translation to operate within relatively stable territory. Therefore, despite a Nabokovian temptation to render the real work over a cosmetic embellishment, I aimed for the inherent relativity between characters, plot, and theme, while striving to transpose three-dimensional attributes of language. For practical purposes I strove to translate the first draft in a Ciceronian style before exploiting cultural and historical associations of individual words and phrases. I tried leaving as few of my fingerprints as possible, for as many times as I turned words over (and over). Romanian—the source language—is replete with more than two thousand years of culture, folklore, history, and as many mysteries as Orpheus and Dionysus combined, since linguistic and historical evidence makes the point that its origins include a significant non-Latin root.

The translatability of the text revealed just how pertinent translation theory was to a play whose action is both spatially and temporally remote. Blaga undertook to translate a significant historical and folkloric component of an indigenous culture, without the luxury of knowing the ancient source language. In addition, he was attempting to access a non-Roman ancestral culture via a Latinized people and language. It is not the present concern of this translation to speculate on the political implications of Blaga's intention at that time, although they are exquisitely present; such integral properties of the play make for fertile discussions in their own right at another time. It is worth noting, however, that such issues of national identity and cultural birthright contribute heavily to the dynamics of the play proper. Part of the myth-making process is, finally, a matter of timing, arrangement and purpose. Not only does Blaga create Zalmoxis as a myth, he does it in a contemporary language of Zalmoxis' posterity—a correctly anticipated maneuver. The fact that he extends and ancient culture to what would be its natural endpoint, reflects Blaga's perception of language as subject to forces of evolution. He manages, hence, to create also a sense of syncretized strangeness in contemporary Romanian, by reinforcing key aspects of oral tradition, not limited to remote metaphor, complex imagery, and extremely inert semiotics. For example, Herodotus tells us that Zalmoxis preached immortality, and at some point sequestered himself in a cave for four years, before returning among his people. Blaga invents the circumstances that shape his play at great risk, no doubt, but he succeeds in providing stunning, yet subtle insight into aspects of Dionysian and orphic mysteries as well. In this fashion, Blaga seems to compensate for the veritable obscurity of the Dacian language, by his haptic and intuitive grasp of the Dacian philosophy on life, community, nature, mythology and spiritual immortality. I too opted for presenting the characters and actions as a philosophical whole, over the exclusive interpretation of linguistic text. This resulted in a translation whose literalness maintains that raw rendering is purer in meaning than a more sophisticated, embellished version. Put another way, I avoided the heresy of interpretation by focusing on Blaga's philosophical framing of the legendary Zalmoxis. What some readers may find awkward in terms of word order or regionalisms, is simply an unapologetic rendering of expression. We are not only traveling across co-temporal languages, but traveling back in time as well. Even Blaga's original Romanian poetic prose, with its odd punctuation and lofty colloquialisms puts the emphasis on the characters' ontology, rather than on linguistic performance.

Consequently, I solved what struck me as a problematic passage in Zalmoxis' opening monologue, and again in Act III, by creating an internal dialogue. Since this is a spoken part, the length might be too heavy on a Western audience. But this artistic innovation actually speaks to my earlier point: the highly reflexive nature of Zalmoxis' lengthy monologue reveals the meditative nature of Blaga's use of philosophy as a dramatic tool. The sense in the original Romanian is just that—an internal dialogue, the kind of auto-dialectic that craves enlightenment. By breaking up the monologue, I came closer to apprehending not only the character of Zalmoxis, but his relationship

Doris C. Plantus

to nature, national identity, and immortality of the human soul. In other places, however, I followed syntactic form and overall structure, complete with Blaga's grammar and punctuation.

Doris C. Plantus

Troy, 2020

Acknowledgments

I think it would be impossible to offer greater praise of Lucian Blaga's play *Zamolxe*, and indeed his entire corpus than to say I inherited the very intuitive prowess of what he came to define as mythosophy long before I discovered his work. As a first-generation Romanian born in the United States, I did not experience an introduction to Blaga as a native; instead, my first exposure came at 16, when I visited Romania and returned with a book of his poems. Soon after, my cousin, Emilia Lazi Kirch sent me a number of books, which included his dramatic poem, *Zamolxe.* Thus I must thank her first, for providing the opportunity for me to know his particular genius.

Also I remain appreciative of Virgil Nemoianu's thoughtful editorial comments.

Finally, I acknowledge the support and enthusiasm of my family, in particular my children, Benjamin and his wife Cristina, and Daniel. They never cease to motivate me even under the most challenging circumstances. Also I thank my father, Deacon Aurel Plantus, and my mother Mary, for giving me the pure essence of my cultural identity, and urging me forward at every turn in my grand journey of fulfillment. Without them, this project would not have been possible.

To everyone who offered constructive criticism, worthwhile suggestions, and the means by which to acquire the necessary contacts in order to complete this task of translation, I thank you with all my heart. Last but not least, a special thank you to Tom Yagiela for his loving support and advice.

PERSOANE

ZAMOLXE, în floarea vîrstei

MAGUL, bătrîn

VRĂJITORUL

CIOPLITORUL GREC

ZEMORA, fiica Magului

CIOBANUL

GHEBOSUL

MOŞNEAGUL

BĂRBATUL

TÎNĂRUL

COPII, OSTAŞI, şi POPOR

Acţiunea se petrece în munţii Daciei

DRAMATIS PERSONAE

ZALMOXIS, in the flower of his age

MAGUS, an old priest

THE SORCERER

THE GREEK WOODCARVER

ZEMORA, Daughter of Magul

THE SHEPHERD

THE HUNCHBACK

THREE APPARITIONS:

     OLD MAN

     YOUNG MAN

     MAN ON THE STAKE

CHILDREN:

    THE SMALLEST CHILD

    THE MIDDLE CHILD

    THE OLDEST CHILD

SOLDIERS

BACCHANTE

DACIAN PEOPLE

The action takes place in the Dacian mountains, cc 1BC.

ACTUL ÎNTÎI

I

O peşteră larg căscată. Multe stînci. Amurg. Un stejar bătrîn cu o
scorbură. Zamolxe, cu o piele de căprioară pe uneri, şade în faţa
peşterii, pe o piatră.

ZAMOLXE
(singur)

Mă-mpărtăşesc cu cîte-un strop din tot ce creşte	1
şi se pierde.	
Nimic nu mi-e strein,	
şi numai marea îmi lipseşte.	
Duhul meu—al meu sau al pămîntului e tot atît—	5
şi-a aşternut aici cojocul său de muşchi şi-aşteaptă.	
De cite ori nu cîntă, el aşteaptă,	
şi visul vine harnic să-l dezmierde.	
Lac îmblînzit de zile fără vînt sunt eu,	
Şi-s singur.	10
Atît de singur că de mult uitat-am să mai fac deosebire	
Între mine şi-ntre lucruri.	

Zalmoxis

Act I

I

A large cave entrance. [1]Many rocks. Dusk. An old hollowed oak tree. Zalmoxis sits on a rock at the mouth of the cave, a deerskin wrapped around his shoulders.

ZALMOXIS

(*alone*)

I make communion with drops of all that thrives   1
and is lost.
Nothing is strange to me,
and only the sea I am missing.
My Spirit—mine and the earth's is just as much as this—   5
and it has spread here its mighty cloak and waits.
Sometimes he sings not, he waits,
and the dream comes heartily to pamper him.
A lake calmed by days without wind, am I,
and I am alone.   10
So alone that I long have I forgotten the difference
between me and things that surround me.

---

[1] Kolgaion is the name of the holy mountain associated with the Getae, as recorded by Strabon, *Geografia,* VII, 3,5.

40

Doris C. Plantus

(*adresîndu-şi spiritul în natură*)

Numai om cu om eşti: tu şi eu.

Singurătatea spălăceşte-aceste mărginiri,   15

Şi împletindu-te cu taina lor, te pierzi în stîncă

Şi te scurgi în unde şi-n pămînt.

Nu ştiu:

Mă-ntorc în mine ori cucernic îmi îndrept

Urechea spre păduri?   20

Aud un glas de mierlă zgomotoasă:

E Dumnezeu?

E Orbul?

Departe eşti poporul meu dac, neam de urşi.

Religie nouă şi vînjoasă încercat-am să-ţi aduc   25

Din inima necunoscutului.

Voiam să-ţi fiu un bun răsad.

Dar tu, neînţelegîndu-mi rostul, mi-ai lovit

Cu pietre vorbele.

A fost o vreme cînd urlam. Voiam să răzvrătesc   30

Şi munţii împotriva ta, şi le strigam:

Rostogoliţi-vă cerurile, nebunia şi apele

Peste mîndria neamului meu trac,—

Ci azi veninul mi s-a potolit,

Şi în zilele-mi făr' de sfîrşit s-a aşezat   35

Un prund de înţelepciune.

Zalmoxis

(addressing his spirit in nature)

Man to man are you: you and I.

Solitude washes away the defining edges,   15

and weaving yourself into their secrets, you lose yourself in the rock

and run off in waves and into the ground.

I do not know:

do I turn inward or, conquering, do I incline my

ear to the forest?   20

I hear the voice of a noisy blackbird:

Is it God?

Is it the Blind One?

Distant are you, my Dacian people, clan of the bear.

A new and robust religion tried I to bring you   25

from the heart of the Unknown One.

I wanted to be a good seedling for you,

but you, knowing not my purpose, you struck

with stones my words.

There was a time when I howled. I wanted to raise   30

even the mountains in mutiny against you, and I called to them:

tumble down your skies, madness and waters

upon the pride of my Thracian brethren—

but today my venom has subsided,

and over my days without end has settled   35

a bedrock of wisdom.

VOCEA LUI ZAMOLXE

E mult de-atunci, mult. Soarele îşi coborîse

Toată mierea în livadă, cînd ţi-am spus

Parabola cu Orbul.

Despre Dumnezeu nu poţi vorbi decît aşa: 40

Îl întrupezi în floare şi-l ridici în palme,

ZAMOLXE

Îl preface în gînd şi-l tăinueşti în suflet,

VOCEA LUI ZAMOLXE

Îl asemeni c-un izvor şi-l laşi să-ţi curgă lin

Peste picioare,

ZAMOLXE

Îl prefaci în soare şi-l aduni cu ochii, 45

îl închipui om şi-l rogi să vie-n sat,

VOCEA LUI ZAMOLXE

Unde îl aşteaptă toate visurile omeneşti,

ZAMOLXE

Arunci grăunţe între brazde şi zici:

VOCEA LUI ZAMOLXE

Din ele creşte Dumnezeu.

ZAMOLXE

În dimineaţa ceea, ca să mă priceapă şi copiii, 50

l-am schimbat în orb.

VOICE OF ZALMOXIS

It is a long time since that time, a long time. The sun had driven down

its honey into the orchard, when I told you

the parable of the Blind One.

You cannot speak of God but in this way: 40

you embody him in a flower and raise him in your palms—

ZALMOXIS

—you conceive him in your mind and make him a mystery in your

soul—

VOICE OF ZALMOXIS

— you perceive him a wellspring and let him run gently

over your feet...

ZALMOXIS

...you make him the sun and gather him with your eyes,   45

you imagine him a man and invite him to your village—

VOICE OF ZALMOXIS

— where every human dream awaits him.

ZALMOXIS

You scatter grains between the furrows and you say:

VOICE OF ZALMOXIS

From these grains grows God.

ZALMOXIS

In that very morning, that even children may understand me,   50

I made him blind.

ZAMOLXE (CONT)

Le-am spus: Noi suntem văzători,

VOCEA LUI ZAMOLXE

Iar Dumnezeu e-un orb bătrîn.

ZAMOLXE

Fiecare e copilul lui—

Şi fiecare îl purtăm de mînă.   55

Căci nu eşti tu Dumnezeire nenţelesul orb,

Ce-şi pipăie cărarea printre spini?

Nu ştii nici tu de unde vii şi unde mergi.

Eşti chinuitul gînd strivit în gol.

Te zbuciumi veşnic dibuind   60

Să faci minuni, cum n-au mai fost,

Dar braţele nu-ţi sunt aşa de tari

Precum ţi-e visul de înalt.

Atît de des tu cazi înfrînt

Şi nici nu bănuieşti furtuna de lumină ce-ai creat-o.   65

Mă strigi?

Mă chemi?

Din fundul unei mări?

Turbărătorul-ţi chiot vine, vine.

VOCEA LUI ZAMOLXE

Iată sunt făptura ta, şi-aici sunt ochii mei, îi vrei?   70

ZALMOXIS (CONT'D)

I told them: "We are the seeing,"

VOICE OF ZALMOXIS

...while God is an old blind man.

ZALMOXIS

Everyone is his child—

and each of us takes him by the hand. 55

For are you not the divine incomprehensible blind one,

who feels his way among the thorns?

Not even you know whence you come nor where you go.

You are the tormented thought crushed in space.

You writhe eternally 60

fumbling to make miracles, as never were before,

but your arms are not as strong

as your dream is lofty.

So often you fall defeated

and never suspect the storm of light you created. 65

Do you cry out to me?

Do you call me?

From the bottom of the sea?

Your turbulent shout comes, it comes.

VOICE OF ZALMOXIS

Behold me, I am your incarnation, and here are my eyes, do you want

them? 70

Doris C. Plantus

VOCEA LUI ZAMOLXE (CONT)

Nu suntem oare pentru ca fără de silă

Să luăm pe micii noştri umeri

Soarta ta puternicule Orb?

ZAMOLXE

Tăcutule, tristule:

Noi mîntuitorii tăi,   75

Noi sălbaticii copii.

De ce mi-au sfîrticat cu pietre gura,

Cînd astfel le vorbisem despre tine

În dimineaţa ceea?

Nu era destul de darnic soarele,   80

Şi gîndurile mele speriau din cuiburi paserile?

Nu eram destul de blind?

De-atunci s-a prăvălit în atîta timp

Şi iezerul cu unda lui mi-a mîngîiat amarul.

Aici sunt aiuritele tăceri   85

Din care poţi privi dosul lumii.

(Se ridică şi din scorbura stejarului scoate un fagure galben. Îl stoarce—

şi mierea curge în nisip.)

O toamnă nouă.

Stupul mi-e sătul şi mierea-i curge de pe buze

Ca laptele din gura unui prunc ce-a supt prea mult.

VOICE OF ZALMOXIS (CONT'D)

Are we not instead meant to take without coercion

upon our small shoulders,

your fate, all powerful Blind One?

ZALMOXIS

Quiet One, Sad One:

 we, your saviors,   75

we, the wild children.

Why did they smash my mouth to bits with stones

when I had spoken this way to them of you

in that morning?

Was not the sun kind enough   80

and were my thoughts frightening the birds from their nests?

Wasn't I gentle enough?

Since then so much time has collapsed

and the mountain lake with its wave comforted my bitterness.

Here are the rambling silences   85

from which you can behold from the backside of the world.

He rises and takes from the hollow of the tree a yellow honeycomb. He
crushes it with his fingers and the honey drips onto the sand.

Oh, new autumn.

My hive is full and its honey drips from the lips

like milk from the mouth of an infant that has sucked too much.

48

ZAMOLXE (CONT)

De-acum amurgurile reci vor face rînd pe rînd   90

Din fiecare frunză de stejar un clopoţel de-aramă,

Iar noaptea vor cădea mai multe stele.

În gura peşterii

Voi sta, în pace să le număr, şi-mi voi zice:

Stele se-ntorc în lume!   95

Dar paşii mei scoţind scîntei din cremene,

Vor mai găsi drumul

Spre cetate,

Spre lume?

VOCEA LUI ZAMOLXE

Rîzînd   100

În templul ei voi arunca seminţe multe

Pentru porumbii Orbului.

Intră în peşteră.

II

Nu departe în fund se văd zidurile cetăţii. În stînga o parte a templului, columne şi trepte jur împrejur. În faţa templului, ceva mai îndărăt, o spînzurătoare. Apus de soare. Ostaşi păzesc templul; ei zac grămadă, numai unul e în picioare pe trepte cu suliţa pe umăr. Doi muncitori întârzie cu cele din urmă lucrări la spînzurătoare.

ZALMOXIS (CONT'D)

From now on the chilly dusks will make one after the other   90

from every oak leaf a bell of brass,

while many more stars will fall at night.

In the mouth of the cave

will I stand quietly, to number them, and I will say to myself:

The stars are returning to the world!   95

But will my footsteps, sparking from where they strike the flint rock

ever find the road that leads

to the fortress,

to the world?

VOICE OF ZALMOXIS

Laughing   100

in their temple I will hurl many seeds

for the doves of the Blind One.

He enters into the cave.

II

The walls of the fortress can be seen mid-stage. On the left is a part of the temple, columns and stairs all around. In front of the temple, off to the side, are gallows. Sunset. Soldiers guard the temple, huddled in a pile. Only one is standing on the steps with a spear resting on his shoulder. Two workers hurry with finishing touches on the gallows.

UN OSTAŞ

(către ostaşul străin)

Unde te-au prins ai noştri?

OSTAŞUL STRĂIN

Lîngă Dunăre.

ALT OSTAŞ

Şi nu ţi-e niciodată dor de ţara ta?   105

OSTAŞUL STRĂIN

O, da. La noi cresc portocali cu fructe roşii;

Zeii nu au coarne boureşti cum cei hrăniţi de voi,

Şi iarna cerul nu roieşte fulgi de nea.

La noi e totul altfel,

Dar soarele se-asemănă aşa de mult cu cel de-aici,   110

c-aproape crezi, ca-i unul şi acelaşşi.

(Toţi rîd)

ÎNTÎIUL OSTAŞ

(către străin)

Tu eşti întîiul sclav care se bucură

De-un slobod trai pe aceste plaiuri.

Vieţuieşti cu aceleiaşi drepturi ca şi noi.

Nu-ţi ştiam prea îndurător stăpînul.   115

Raspunde, libertatea cum ţi-ai dobîndit-o?

FIRST SOLDIER

(*addressing a foreign soldier*)

Where did our people capture you?

FOREIGN SOLDIER

By the Danube.

SECOND SOLDIER

Don't you ever miss your own country?   105

FOREIGN SOLDIER

Yes, of course. In our country orange trees grow with red fruit;

the gods have not the horns of oxen like those you raise,

and in the winter, the sky swarms not with snow.

In our land everything is different,

but the sun is so much like yours   110

that you would think they are one and the same.

Everyone laughs.

FIRST SOLDIER

(*to the foreign soldier*)

You are the first slave who rejoices

over a liberated life on these plains.

Why, you have the same rights as we do.

We didn't know your merciful master, though.   115

Tell us, how did you win your freedom?

OSTAŞUL STRĂIN

(şiret)

Cu...opincile profetului...

CEILALŢI

Cu ce? Haide, spune, povesteşte!

OSTAŞUL STRĂIN

E mult de cînd gonirăţi pe Zamolxe?

ÎNTÎIUL OSTAŞ

Vreo cîţiva ani.   120

OSTAŞUL STRĂIN

Ei bine, mucenicii lui se tot sporesc de-atunci

Pe sub pămînt ca iepurii de casă.

Altfel de ce-am păzi noi templul zi şi noapte?

Magul se înspăimîntă de puterea lor, şi precum ştiţi,

Făgăduit-a chiar pe fiica lui ca dar sălbatic   125

Celui ce va da de urma lui Zamolxe.

Ori aţi uitat?

AL DOILEA OSTAŞ

Ehei, Zemora tulburătoarea! Cîţi n-o doresc!

OSTAŞUL STRĂIN

(zîmbind a gluma)

Cum eu trăiam mai mult din mila cînilor.

Mă hotărîi să caut ascunzişul lui Zamolxe.   130

Am iscodit prin munţi. Vreo nouă zile ostenitu-m-am

FOREIGN SOLDIER

(*cunningly*)

With...the prophet's slippers....

SEVERAL SOLDIERS

With what? Come then, tell us the story!

FOREIGN SOLDIER

How long has it been since you chased Zalmoxis away?

FIRST SOLDIER

A few years.   120

FOREIGN SOLDIER

That's good. His followers are thriving

beneath the earth like rabbits in the yard.

Otherwise, why would we be watching the temple day and night?

Magus is terrified of their strength, and as you all know,

he has promised his daughter as a wild gift   125

to the one who uncovers Zalmoxis' tracks.

Or have you forgotten?

SECOND SOLDIER

Ah-ha, the wild Zemora! Who doesn't desire her?

FOREIGN SOLDIER

(*smiling at the joke*)

Living a sorrowful life as I was, mostly by the kindness of dogs,

caused me to seek the hiding place of Zalmoxis.   130

I searched him out in the mountains. I sought him wearily for nine days

OSTAŞUL STRĂIN (CONT)

Prin văgăuni, dar n-am găsit

Decît nişte opinci întortocheate. Mi-am zis:

Sunt ale profetului! — Le-am dăruit preotului.

E adevărat, îi aduceam numai opincile,   135

Nu capul lui Zamolxe, — cu toate acestea

Îmi hrăneam nădejdea — că de nu-mi dă

Pe Zemora pentru totdeauna de soţie, îmi va da-o

Pentr-o noapte cel puţin. Ce? Frumoasă sărbătoare!

Dar Magul fu zgîrcit şi-mi dete   140

Doar această zdreanţă — de libertate.

Ieri m-a întrebat: cînd îmi aduci şi capul lui Zamolxe?

I-am zis: cînd şi-l va pierde ca opincile, Sfinţia ta!

OSTAŞUL DE STRAJĂ

Răspuns cuminte,

Dar mai bine rămîneai tot sclav   145

Decît să străjuieşti cu noi viclene temple

Văduvite de credinţă.

De lene ni se-ngraşă tălpile pe aceste sfinte lespezi.

Unde-s vremile ce răsunau din bucium către soare?

Prin cîlţi de codri altădată săgetam   150

Bourii între coarne.

AL TREILEA OSTAŞ

Şi pescuiam din fluvii somni rotunzi

Ca pulpele fecioarelor.

AL PATRULEA OSTAŞ

(către cel de strajă)

FOREIGN SOLDIER (CONT'D)

in the backwoods, but I found nothing

but his curled up slippers. I said to myself:

these are the prophet's! I made a gift of them to the priest.

It's true, I brought him only the slippers,   135

not the head of Zalmoxis—but regardless

I nurtured my hope—that even if he didn't give me

Zemora for my wife forever, at least

for one night. So what? A beautiful holiday!

But Magus had been too stingy to give me   140

anything but this rag—of liberty.

Yesterday he asked me: when will you bring me the head of Zalmoxis?

I answered: when he loses it like his slippers, your holiness!

SOLDIER ON WATCH

A wise response,

But better you should have remained a slave   145

instead of guarding the temple with a cunning lot like us

widowed of faith.

Our soles grow fat from laziness on these hallowed gravestones.

Where, when the sound of the trumpet aimed toward the sun?

And through the flaxen stubble out arrows flew   150

between the horns of oxen?

THE THIRD SOLDIER

and the catfish we pulled from the brooks were as round

as the calves of maidens.

THE FOURTH SOLDIER

(addressing the soldier on watch)

AL PATRULEA OSTAŞ (CONT)

Uite funia spînzurătorii cum o mişcă vîntul —

Îţi face semn! 155

AL CINCILEA OSTAŞ

Răbdare, nu cîrtiţi, copii, răbdare.

Cînd se mişcă vrăjmaşul la hotare,

Ne vom urni puhoi urlînd spre mare

Şi Magul o să uite de altare.

OSTAŞUL DE STRAJĂ

Ghiciţi, băieţi, ghicitoarea mea: sunt fiinţe 160

Ce nu-s aievea,

Şi totuşi omul le păzeşte de primejdii!

De ce? — ca omul, tot el, să aibă de la cine

În primejdie fiind, să ceară ajutor...

AL ŞAPTELEA OSTAŞ

Ghicitoarea ta e ciută de-nţeles. 165

AL OPTULEA OSTAŞ

Ba nu. Aceştia-s zeii!

AL NOULEA OSTAŞ

Le cerem ajutor.

ÎNTIUL OSTAŞ

Şi totuşi noi le ţinem pază de tîlhari,

Noi cu suliţele noastre.

FOURTH SOLDIER (CONT'D)

Look at how the hangman's noose sways in the wind—

it gives you a sign! 155

THE FIFTH SOLDIER

Patience, don't grumble, children, patience.

When the enemy moves about us

we will send a howling torrent to the sea

and Magus will forget about his altars.

SOLDIER ON WATCH

Guess my riddle, boys: there are beings 160

that are not real,

yet a man protects them from dangers!

Why? So that very man can have from whom to beg

for help in times of danger...

THE SEVENTH SOLDIER

Yours is a beast of a riddle to understand. 165

THE EIGHTH SOLDIER

On the contrary. These are gods.

THE NINTH SOLDIER

We ask for their help.

THE FIRST SOLDIER

And still we watch over them and keep thieves at bay

with our spears.

OSTAŞUL DE STRAJĂ

(batjocuritor)

Şi ei — nici măcar nu sunt!— ha, ha! 170

AL DOILEA OSTAŞ

(către cel de strajă)

Nu eşti şi tu unul dintre "orbii" lui Zamolxe?

AL TREILEA OSTAŞ

Linişte! Magul iese din altar.

(Toţi se aşează în două rînduri. Magul trece printre suliţi şi-i priveşte ager în ochi.)

MAGUL

(aspru)

Corbi vreau să văd în zori pe furci!

Aţi înţeles?

La noapte. 175

Nu cruţaţi pe nimeni.

(Dispare în dosul templului. Ostaşii se închină şi s-aşază la locurile lor.)

AL PATRULEA OSTAŞ

Înaltul Preot ţi se sfredeleşte cu privirea

Pînă-n ochii gîndului.

AL CINCELEA OSTAŞ

Bătrînul Mag! N-aţi auzit? Pe cînd cîntau cocoşii

A plecat spre miazăzi cu fiica lui. S-a-ntors tîrziu. 180

SOLDIER ON WATCH

(*making fun*)

And they aren't even real! Ha-ha!   170

THE SECOND SOLDIER

(*addressing the soldier on watch*)

Aren't you one of Zalmoxis' "blind ones" too?

THE THIRD SOLDIER

Quiet! The Mag is coming out of the altar.

(*Everyone assembles into two lines. Magus walks among the spears and looks with agile eyes.*)

MAGUS

(*sharply*)

I want to see ravens on your pitchforks at dawn!

Have you understood?

Tonight.   175

Spare no one.

(*Magus disappears in the back of the temple.*)

THE FOURTH SOLDIER

The high priest has such a piercing look

he can see through to your thoughts.

THE FIFTH SOLDIER

Old Magus! Didn't you hear? While the cocks were still singing

he left with his daughter. He returned late.   180

AL CINCELEA OSTAŞ (CONT)

Fără de ea. Ce-i drept, frumoasă-e, iar furia "orbilor"

E mare; de frica lor

o fi ascuns-o undeva departe în munţii păstratori

De taine şi comori.

AL ŞASELEA OSTAŞ

Spun oameni că el nu doarme niciodată.

AL ŞAPTELEA OSTAŞ

În întuneric ochii lui se văd ca ochi de lupi,   185

Tăciuni aprinşi în vînt.

AL OPTULEA OSTAŞ

(misterios)

Magul e tăcut.

AL NOULEA OSTAŞ

Magul e rece.

ÎNTIUL OSTAŞ

Statornic ca un obicei rămas din zilele strămoşilor.

AL DOILEA OSTAŞ

Setos de sînge ca o fiară.   190

OSTAŞUL DE STRAJĂ

(izbucneşte)

Mai mult decît o fiară. Setos de singe ca învătăturile

Sfinte de astăzi şi din toate vremile.

THE FIFTH SOLDIER (CONT'D)

Without her. It's true, beautiful is she, but the fury of the "blind ones"

is great; for fear of them

he would have hidden her far off in the mountain keep

of secrets and treasure.

THE SIXTH SOLDIER

People say he never sleeps.   185

THE SEVENTH SOLDIER

In the darkness he has the eyes of a wolf,

glowing embers in the wind.

THE EIGHTH SOLDIER

(*mysteriously*)

Magus is silent.

THE NINTH SOLDIER

Magus is cold.

THE FIRST SOLDIER

Steadfast as a tradition left from the days of our forefathers.   190

THE SECOND SOLDIER

Bloodthirsty as a beast.

SOLDIER ON WATCH

(*bursts out*)

More than a beast. Bloodthirsty as the holy lessons

of today and all times.

Doris C. Plantus

OSTAŞUL STRĂIN

Ce roşu-i cerul.

AL PATRULEA OSTAŞ

Şi spînzurătoarea-i gată.   195

OSTAŞUL STRĂIN

(privind spre temple)

Prieteni,

Ne pîndeşte o noapte grozavă —

Din temple — furiş — a ieşit un motan,

Semn rău.

AL CINCELEA OSTAŞ

Motanul cu ochi verzi ca ai Magulului.   200

Prindeţi-l, prindeţi-l!

Legaţi-i cu funia stîrvul de furci

Să se sperie toţi răzvrătiţii!

OSTAŞUL DE STRAJĂ

(izbucneşte într-un hohot şi se întoarce spre temple)

Ha, ha!

O, zei,   205

Mucegăiţi de veşnicie!

Nu-i nici un pumn încleştat

Să dărîme minciuna cu stîlpii de piatră?

Al morţilor poate!

Ieşiţi îngropaţii de vii în pămînt—   210

Şi noi azvîrliţi pe rîuri!

Eu, unul din cei ce rămîn credincioşi

FOREIGN SOLDIER

How red is the sky...

THE SECOND SOLDIER

and the gallows are ready.   195

FOREIGN SOLDIER

(*looking toward the temple*)

Friends,

a dreadful night stalks us—

a tom cat sneaks out from the temple—

a bad sign.

THE FIFTH SOLDIER

A tom cat with green eyes like those of Magus'.   200

Catch him! Catch him!

Tie his carcass to the pitchfork with a rope

so we can frighten all the rebels!

SOLDIER ON WATCH

(*bursts out laughing and turns back toward the temple*)

Ha-ha!

O gods,   205

moldy with eternity!

Is there not one tight fist

to smash the lie with stone columns?

Among the dead perhaps!

Come out you who have been buried alive—   210

 and you who have been cast upon rivers!

I, one of Zalmoxis' remaining faithful

OSTAŞUL DE STRAJĂ (CONT)

lui Zamolxe, vă chem din adînc:

Prăbuşiţi sanctuarul!

O, zei, apăraţi cu pisici spînzurate, 215

mi-e scîrbă.

C-o lance ţintită în porţile voastre

Mă-nchin,

Eu sunt omul—

Ha, ha, — vă salut! 220

(Aruncă lancea în poarta templului. Ceilalţi sar şi-l doboară cu lovituri de suliţi.)

III

Bordeiul unui vrăjitor. Noapte. Pe vatră arde focul. Flăcările luminează întreg bordeiul. Vrăjitorul are pe frunte coarne trace.

VRAJITORUL

(Ia dintr-un ungher un craniu omenesc, toarnă dintr-un ulcior vin în el şi-l aşază pe vatră lîngă flăcări. S-aud lovituri în uşă.)

Cine e?

O VOCE

Magul.

(Vrăjitorul deschide.)

SOLDIER ON WATCH (CONT'D)

summon you forth from the deep:

lay siege to the sanctuary!

O, gods, shielded by strangled kittens.   215

I am disgusted.

With my spearpoint aimed at your gates

I bow down,

I am the man—

ha-ha—I salute you!   220

He hurls his spear at the temple door. The others quickly jump on him and beat him down with their spear handles.

.

III

A sorcerer's cottage. Night, Fire burns in the hearth. The flames light up the inside. The sorcerer wears Thracian horns.

SORCERER

(*He takes from a corner a human skull, and fills it with wine from a jug. Loud pounding is heard at the door and he sets the skull down on the hearth.*)

Who is it?

MAGUS

Magus.

The Sorcerer opens the door and lets him in.

MAGUL

(intre gîfîind)

Dă-mi adăpost sub straşina puterii tale.Nu de tunete,

Dar de năpîrci.

S-au răsculat învăţăceii lui Zamolxe.   225

Un zvon trecu spre seară prin cetate

Că m-aşteaptă gîrla-n noaptea asta.

VRAJITORUL

Şi templul?

MAGUL

Îl străjuiesc ostaşi voinici.

VRAJITORUL

Voinici or fi, dar sunt şi credincioşi?   230

MAGUL

(se mai linişteşte.)

Ca fumul de tămîie.

VRAJITORUL

S-a-ntors Zamolxe?

MAGUL

De cînd fugi, nu i-au mai dat de urmă.

Spun unii că s-a prăpădit stingher prin munţi,

Dar alţii mai şoptesc că va să vie iaraşi   235

Să-mi smulgă templul şi să sfarme zeii.

MAGUS

(*rushing in out of breath*)

Give me shelter beneath the roof of your power. Not from thunder,

but from vipers.

Zalmoxis' disciples have risen up.   225

Word travels through the fortress

that the throng awaits me this night.

SORCERER

And the temple?

MAGUS

The hearty soldiers keep watch over it.

SORCERER

Hearty they may be, but are they faithful?   230

MAGUS

(*growing calmer*)

Like the smoke from the incense.

SORCERER

Has Zalmoxis returned?

MAGUS

Ever since he ran off, they haven't found his trail.

Some say that he has become a lonely wretch in the mountains,

but others whisper that he will surely come again   235

to snatch the temple away from me and smash the gods.

VRAJITORUL

Sunt tocmai şapte ani de cînd ai îndîrjit

Mulţimea să-l alunge.

Eu nu te-am sfătuit, căci un profet

Nu e nimic, dar un profet lovit— e mult.   240

MAGUL

(scîrbit)

Poporul, poporul!

VRAJITORUL

Ce sfînta-ar fi prostia lui de n-ar fi schimbăcioasă!

MAGUL

(dezămăgit)

Amară de-ntrebări mi-e inima. Zeii, cum ni-i vom scăpa?

Cum, o cum îi vom scăpa?

Eu—pîndarul veşniciei—cad.   245

VRAJITORUL

Zeii se hrănesc cu suflet omenesc.

Cînd se isprăveşte-acest nutreţ,

Cînd nu mai crede nimenea în ei,

s-adună trişti şi-şi cheamă marele sfîrşit.

Nu le poate ajuta nici mierea   250

Şi nici laptele de capre.

Laptele de capre, care fără de-a fi muls,

Se scurge pentru ei prin buruieni cînd ugerele

Sunt prea pline.

SORCERER

It is actually seven years since you persuaded

the people to cast him out.

I didn't advise, because a prophet

is nothing, but a prophet struck down—is great. 240

MAGUS

(disgusted)

The people! The people!

SORCERER

How holy would his stupidity be if he weren't so fickle!

MAGUS

(despairingly)

My heart is bitter with questions. The gods—how will they save us?

How, o how will we save them?

I—the keeper of eternity—fall. 245

SORCERER

The gods feed on the human soul.

When this nutrient has been depleted,

when all cease to believe in them,

they gather sadly, and call for their great end.

Neither honey, nor goat's milk shall help them. 250

Goat's milk,

if it is not milked

runs over the weeds for them when their udders

are too full.

Doris C. Plantus

MAGUL

(ridică braţele)

Nemuritorilor, vă zvîntă necredinţa!　　　255

De nicăieri nu vă mijeşte mîntuirea!

Zadarnic ani m-am zvîrcolit atîţia-n neodihnă.

Răspunsul

Nu mi l-au dat nici tablele

Înţelepciunii negre aduse din Egipet,　　　260

Nici amintirea sibilinicelor sfaturi

Auzite-n fumul de la Delfi.

VRAJITORUL

Nici cea mai naltă dintre multele virtuţi?

MAGUL

(îşi adună gîndurile)

Viclenia?

VRAJITORUL

Izvorul nesecat de bune sfaturi.　　　265

Vino, liniştete-te. Răspunsul căutat va trebui

Să-ţi bată într-o zi la poartă—

Dacă astazi nu, atuncea mîine.

Credinţa veche n-o să moară:

Un butuc de vie crezi de mult uscat　　　270

Şi totuşi toamn îl găseşti mai încărcat

De struguri decît orişicînd.

Să ne-aşezăm în pîlpîirea vetrei. Eşti obosit?

Răbdare.

În adăpostul meu e cald.　　　275

MAGUS

(*raising his arms*)

You, undead, your faithlessness dries up!   255

Your salvation blinks from nowhere!

For years have I tossed restlessly and in vain.

The answer

Not even the black tablets

of wisdom brought forth from Egypt gave me,   260

not even the Sibyll's recollection of advice

heard in the smoke at Delphi.

SORCERER

Not even the highest of virtues?

MAGUS

(*collecting his thoughts*)

Deceit?

SORCERER

The eternal spring of advice.   265

Come, calm yourself. The answer you seek will have

to knock on your door one day—

if not today, then tomorrow.

The old faith will not die:

a trunk of the grape vine you think long dry   270

is even more laden than ever

with grapes than ever in autumn.

Let us sit near the flickering hearth. Are you tired?

Have patience.

In my shelter it is warm.   275

VRĂJITORUL (CONT)

Aşa. Şi-acuma înc-odată: viclenia!

MAGUL

(luminîndu-se dintr-o dată)

Un gînd, bătrînule, un gînd.

Ascultă- mă Nu-s singur. Tu-mi eşti bun.

Tu nu m-ai părăsit.

Să-ntindem în ascuns poporului o cursă?   280

Mulţimei să-i lăsăm nălucă.

Religia lui Zamolxe-şi face cuib acum

Şi-n inimile cele mai statornice prin vechile ogaşe.

El nu s-a întors şi totuşi e aci.

El ne doboară zeii pentru Orbul său.   285

Ce-ar fi să răspîndim povestea în popor,

Că Zamolxe a fost un zeu el însuşi?

Ce pierdem?

Avem un zeu mai mult în primitorul nostru templu,

Dar astfel mîntuim întreg soborul zeilor.   290

Oamenii divinizînd pe Zamolxe

Îi vor uita învăţătura.

VRĂJITORUL

O cursă vrednică de isteţimea unui mag.

Legendă făcătoare de minuni: ce solzi strălucitori,

Şireată, ochi de şarpe.   295

Oamenii divinizînd pe Zamolxe îi vor uita învăţătura.

E gîndul tău? O mare Preot.

SORCERER (CONT'D)

So. And once again: deceit!

MAGUS
(*brightening suddenly*)

A thought, old one, a thought.

Listen to me. I'm not alone. You are good for me.

You haven't abandoned me.

Shall we spread a curse secretly among the people?   280

We should give the people a ghost.

Zalmoxis' religion is now making itself a nest

in the hearts of the most faithful through the old quarters.

He hasn't returned and yet he is here.

He smashes our gods for his Blind One.   285

So, how would it be if we spread the story among the people

that Zalmoxis, himself, was a god;

What have we to lose?

For the price of one extra god in our gracious temple,

we will save the whole pantheon of gods.   290

As the people begin to worship Zalmoxis,

they will soon forget his teachings.

SORCERER

A worthy trap from the wisdom of a magician.

A legend- maker of miracles. What sparkling scales,

crafty, snake eyes.   295

People will deify Zalmoxis—and they will forget his teachings.

Is this your idea? Oh, great priest.

Doris C. Plantus

MAGUL

Nu-i nimenea-n bordei?

Ţi-e uşa bine zăvorîtă?

VRĂJITORUL

Să nu ai nici o teamă. 300

MAGUL

Ogoru-i proaspăt

Şi legenda va întinde rădăcini.

Poporul va striga:

Să aşezăm statuia lui Zamolxe-n temple

Între ceilalţi zei, cum se cuvine. 305

Cînd nu mai e nici o putere

Să-nfrîngă-nvăţătura unui nou profet,

Un singur lucru e mai tare ca profetul:

Statuia lui!

Dă-mi mîna ta şi prietenia gîndurilor tale! 310

VRĂJITORUL

(îi întinde mîna)

Mîna şi cuvîntul meu!

MAGUL

(încet)

De tine-ascultă apa!

VRĂJITORUL

(mai încet)

De mine-ascultă focul!

75

MAGUS

There is no one else in your cottage?

Is your door bolted shut?

SORCERER

Have no fear.   300

MAGUS

The field is fresh

and the legend will stretch forth its roots.

The people will shout:

Let us place the statue of Zalmoxis in the temple

among the other gods, as it is fitting.   305

When there is no more strength left

to harness the teachings of a new prophet,

a single thing is more powerful than the prophet himself:

his statue!

Give me your hand, and the friendship of your thoughts!   310

SORCERER

(*extending his hand*)

My hand and my word!

MAGUS

(*softly*)

Even the water obeys you!

SORCERER

(*quieter still*)

Even the fire obeys me!

MAGUL

De tine-ascultă vîntul!

VRĂJITORUL

De mine-ascultă stelele!   315

MAGUL

Şi mai presus de orişice

De tine-ascultă tot ce nu e.

VRĂJITORUL

Eu ştiu vrăji poveştile să se prefacă-n adevăr.

MAGUL

Ţi-am dat povestea.

VRĂJITORUL

Eu ţi adaug descîntecul.   320

MAGUL

(*tresare*)

Un zgomot surd lîngă bordei.

VRĂJITORUL

Doar paşii ai liniştei. N-aud nimic.

MAGUL

Ura lor m-adulmecă. Deschide uşa şi ascultă!

MAGUS

Even the wind obeys you!

SORCERER

Even the stars obey me!   315

MAGUS

Above all things,

even all that is not obeys you.

SORCERER

I know how to bewitch stories so that they become truth.

MAGUS

I gave you the story.

SORCERER

I will add the spell.   320

MAGUS

(*startled*)

A muted sound near the cottage.

SORCERER

It's only the footfall of silence. I hear nothing.

MAGUS

Their hatred tracks my scent. Just open the door and listen!

VRĂJITORUL

(deschide—apoi, c-un strigăt)

Arde cetatea!

(amîndoi sar în prag)

MAGUL

(furtunos)

Pîrjol spre miazăzi.   325

Încăierare. Vîlvătaie. Templul e departe,

Nu-l vor cuceri. O, numai cerul să nu ardă.

Alte flăcări.

Taci,

Ascultă!   330

VRĂJITORUL

E plîns îndepărtat.

MAGUL

Mi-au dat de urmă.

VRĂJITORUL

Sunt paseri speriate: îşi scutură funinginea

Şi spuza de pe aripi.

MAGUL

Pîn-aici aduce vîntul scrumul.   335

(Amîndoi se retrag speriaţi. La un semn al Vrăjitorului—Magul se ascunde în pămînt lîngă vatră. Vrăjitorul pune vreascuri pe focul care stă se stingă. După cîteva clipe, apare.)

Zalmoxis

SORCERER

(*opens the door and lets out a yell*)

The fortress is burning!

(*Both leap into the doorway.*)

MAGUS

(*angrily*)

Calamity in the south.   325

A siege. Flames. The temple is far,

they will not overtake it. O, only that the sky should not burn.

Other flames.

Quiet,

listen!   330

SORCERER

A weeping in the distance.

MAGUS

They have tracked me.

SORCERER

'Tis only frightened birds: they are shaking the soot

and hot ash from their wings.

MAGUS

The wind brings the ashes all the way here.   335

They both withdraw, shaken. The Sorcerer gives Magus a sign to hide in the cellar, near the hearth. Then the sorcerer puts kindling on the fire that is about to go out. After a few moments, the Shepherd appears.

CIOBANUL

(cu cojoc de oaie, înfăţişare bolnavă, aiurînd)

Mîine iar răsare luna—

mi-e frică de lumina ei.

Soarele e uşor, dar luna-i grea.

Cînd mă atinge pe pleope, cad trăsnit

Ca de-o măciucă-n frunte, şi mă schimb   340

În priculici. Oriunde-aş fi, în munţi,

pe o muche aşteptînd, sau fluierînd în stînă,

cad—şi-n chip de fiară neagră-mi sfîşiu

oile din turmă.

Auzii din trecători că tu ştii leacuri,   345

Cari te vindecă de lună.

VRĂJITORUL

De cînd îţi porţi osînda?

CIOBANUL

E-al şaptelea cules de vii.

Neastîmpărata droiae asculta-n livada Orbului

Cuvîntul lui Zamolxe.   350

Am fost întîiul care l-am brodat c-o piatră

În obraz. Ne aţîţase Magul.

Nu mai ştiu, am tremurat apoi şi mă durea,

Caci tînărul deschise ochii mari şi trişti—

Şi n-a-ntrebat de ce.   355

Dar în aceiaşi seară s- ivit şi luna.

Mi-am sfîrticat cinci oi şi am plîns în lîna lor,

De-atunci prin rouă, brumă, ploi, lau cîmpii-n goană tot la fel.

SHEPHERD

(*He is wearing a sheep skin coat and has a delirious countenance.*)

Tomorrow the moon rises again—

I am afraid of her light.

The sun is light, but the moon is heavy.

When it touches my eyelids, I fall

as though struck with a club on my forehead, and I change   340

into werewolf. No matter where I am, on the mountains

waiting on a ridge, or whistling in the sheepfold,

I fall—and in the form of a black beast I rent

the sheep from my own flock.

I heard from passersby that you have remedies   345

that can cure me of the moon-sickness.

SORCERER

Since when do you bear this curse?

SHEPHERD

The seventh harvest of the grapes.

The uneasy throng had gathered in the orchard of the Blind One

to listen to Zalmoxis speak.   350

I was the first one to strike him with a rock

in the face. Magul had taunted us.

I don't know anymore, I trembled and after I ached

because the young man opened his sad eyes, wide—

and did not ask why.   355

But on this same night the moon had appeared also.

I tore five sheep to shreds and then I wept in their fleece.

Ever since through dew, frost, rain, I take the fields full speed the same.

CIOBANUL (CONT)

Mă duc pe urmele acelui tînăr cu ochi mari

Şi caut în nisipuri sîngele ce-a curs din trupul său.   360

Cînd sorb o picătură, mă dezmeticesc

Şi iaraşi mă fac—om.

VRĂJITORUL

Din slava mai presus de fire voi plivi

Misterul lui Zamolxe.

Nu eşti întîiul care suferă pe urma lui,   365

Străinule!

CIOBANUL

Păzeşte-mă de lună.

VRĂJITORUL

(*aruncă bobi de tămîie în flăcări şi apoi ridică mîna deasupra focului*)

Tu, cel ce vezi prin lucruri,

Duh al vetrelor,

Jeratic al amurgului,   370

Destăinuieşte-te îm graiul tău de flăcări!

VOCEA MAGULUI

(*din pămînt—misterios*)

Zamolxe n-a fost om.

CIOBANUL

Păzeşte-mă de lună.

SHEPHERD

I track the young man with the big eyes

and seek in the sand the blood that runs from his body.   360

When I sip a drop of his spilled blood I come to my senses

and become once more—a man.

SORCERER

By the glory of a superior grace will I weed out

the mystery of Zalmoxis.

You are not the first to suffer in his wake,   365

Stranger!

SHEPHERD

Protect me from the moon.

SORCERER

(tosses nuggets of incense into the flames, raising his hand with great

ceremony)

You, the one who sees through things,

spirit of the hearth,

ember of the twilight,   370

reveal yourself in your language of flames.

VOICE OF MAGUS

(mysteriously, from the ground)

Zalmoxis was not a man.

SHEPHERD

Protect me from the moon.

VOCEA MAGULUI

(din pămînt)

Zamolxe n-a fost om.

VRĂJITORUL

Tu vezi prin lucruri şi prin inimi. 375

VOCEA MAGULUI

Zamolxe n-a fost om. A fost un zeu.

Din cuibul veşniciei

s-a coborît pe trepte de lumină

să vă-nveţe tinereţea şi durerea.

Pîine nu i-aţi dat— 380

Şi piatra strigă.

VRĂJITORUL

Nemuritorii cuibăresc pe-un munte

Ridicat din sori.

Zamolxe nu se-ntoarce înapoi în cerul său?

VOCEA MAGULUI

El n-are nici un sanctuar un chip cioplit 385

Cum se cuvine unui zeu.

Cît nimenea nu i se-nchină,

Zamolxe e legat de lut.

Primejdii va trimite-n suflete,

Pămîntul va scrîşni din stînci, 390

Iar mieii vor pieri ca strugurii din vii.

Ciopl.iţi-i chip de piatră lui Zamolxe!

Zeul strigă, cere jertfe!

Zalmoxis

VOICE OF MAGUS

(from the ground)

Zalmoxis was not a man.

SORCERER

You see through things and through hearts.   375

VOICE OF MAGUS

Zalmoxis was not a man. He was a god.

From the nest of eternity

he descended upon steps of light

to teach you youth and pain.

Bread you did not give him—   380

and the stone cries out.

SORCERER

The deathless nest on a mountain

lifted out of daybreak.

Will not Zalmoxis return to his sky?

VOICE OF MAGUS

He has no sanctuary, nothing carved in his image   385

as would befit a god.

So long as no one worships him

Zalmoxis is bound in clay.

He will send dangers into your souls,

rocks will grind the earth,   390

while lambs will perish like the grapes of the vines.

Carve a body of stone for Zalmoxis!

The god calls out, he asks for sacrifice!

VRĂJITORUL

(ia craniul de pe vatră şi-l poartă prin flăcări)

Apari duh nevăzut în murmurul de flăcări,

Şi mîntuie lunaticii de chin.   395

Tot sîngele vărsat din trupul lui Zamolxe

Adune-se-n aceste picături de vin!

(de trei ori)

VOCEA MAGULUI

Tu eşti stăpînul meu.

(Ciobanul, care tot timpul a ascultat, cade în genunchi.)

VRĂJITORUL

(îi dă băutura vrăjită din craniu)

Jucînd pe creştete

Sub brazi înalţi   400

Îţi va ieşi din cale luna.

Şi luna va să-ţi toarne

Prietenie din suflet—

Moale, dulce, blîndă şi duioasă.

Oile n-or mai avea de tine teamă—   405

Şi nici cîinii tăi.

Închină-te de-acuma mai vîrtos

Acelui zeu pe care l-ai lovit,

Şi adu-i păstrăvi pe altar

Ca un sfielnic sfînt pescar.   410

SORCERER

(takes the skull from the hearth and passes it through the flames)

Show yourself, unseen spirit, in the murmuring flames,

and cure the lunatics of their suffering.   395

May all the blood spilled from Zalmoxis' body

gather in these drops of wine!

(Three times.)

VOICE OF MAGUS

You are my master.

(The shepherd, who has been listening all this time now falls to his

knees.)

SORCERER

(gives the skull with the potion to the shepherd to drink.)

Playing on the crests

beneath the tall pines   400

the moon will cross your path.

And the moon would want to pour

friendship into your soul—

soft, sweet, mild, and tender.

The sheep will no longer fear you—   405

neither will your dogs.

Bow down more virtuously than ever before to

this god whom you struck.

and bring trout upon his altar

like a humbled fisherman.   410

Doris C. Plantus

ACTUL AL DOILEA

I

O livadă înconjurată de vii împrăştiate pe dealuri. Pădure la dreapta. În livadă, vase mari de pamînt pline de must. Culegători vin şi trec cu hîrdaie. Lîngă pădure, Ghebosul, încărcat cu struguri din cale-afară mari, în mîni, pe umeri, stă de vorbă cu un trecător—fără a fi auzit. Mai în faţă, alţi trei culegători povestesc cu ochii îndreptaţi spre Ghebos.

ÎNTÎIUL CULEGĂTOR

Ăsta-i Ghebosul?

AL DOILEA CULEGĂTOR

Da.

AL TREILEA CULEGĂTOR

Mirarea de-aşa rod?
A îngropat sub fiecare viţă cîte-un stîrv de om
Găsit pe drumuri ori pe ape.   5

AL DOILEA CULEGĂTOR

E-adevărat că ştie deochia şi piţigoii de pe ramuri?

ÎNTÎIUL CULEGĂTOR

Nu-i bine să-l priveşti prea mult:

89

ACT II

I

An orchard surrounded by vineyards scattered on the hills. A forest on
the right. In the orchard, many large amphorae filled with fermenting
wine. Harvesters come and go with jugs. Next to the woods, the
Hunchback, loaded down with wonderfully large grapes, in his hands,
on his shoulders, talks to a passerby so that no one can hear him.
Further upstage, another three harvesters chat among themselves, with
their eyes on the Hunchback.

FIRST HARVESTER

This is the hunchback?

SECOND HARVESTER

Yes.

THIRD HARVESTER

Isn't this fruit a marvel?
Beneath every vine trunk the hunchback has buried a corpse
he has found on the road or in the water.   5

THE SECOND HARVESTER

Is it true that he also knows how to charm the finches off the
branches?

FIRST HARVESTER

It's not good to gaze upon him too much;

Doris C. Plantus

ÎNTÎIUL CULEGĂTOR (CONT)

Îţi putrezesc ochii.

AL DOILEA CULEGĂTOR

E numai oase.

Şi tot nu vrea să moară.   10

AL TREILEA CULEGĂTOR

Nici n-o să moară-aşa curînd.

De-l părăseşte sufletul, el fură pe-al vecinului.

Cu sufletul furat—tîlharul

Mai trăieşte-apoi un veac de om.

(Ghebosul se apropie de ei.)

ÎNTÎIUL CULEGĂTOR

(către Ghebos)

Ai un cules atît de bun. Nu-ţi latri   15

Psalmul tău de bucurie? Ha-u, ha-u!

GHEBOSUL

N-am cui să-i mulţumesc.

AL DOILEA CULEGĂTOR

Nici celor îngropaţi sub viţe?

GHEBOSUL

De ce? Fiindcă ei îşi încălzesc la soare sîngele

Urcîndu-se-n lăstarii vieii mele?   20

FIRST HARVESTER (CONT'D)

your eyes will rot.

SECOND HARVESTER

He's just skin and bones.

And still he doesn't want to die. 10

THIRD HARVESTER

He won't die anytime soon, either.

If his soul leaves him, he simply steals his neighbor's.

With a stolen soul— the thief

lives yet another man's lifetime.

(The Hunchback comes near them.)

FIRST HARVESTER

(To the Hunchback)

What a splendid crop you have. Will you not bark 15

your psalm of happiness then? Ha-u, ha-u.

THE HUNCHBACK

I have no one to thank.

SECOND HARVESTER

Not even to those buried beneath your vines?

THE HUNCHBACK

Why? Because they warm their blood

climbing up in the shoots of my grapevines? 20

ÎNTÎIUL CULEGĂTOR

Din atît belşug de struguri nu aduci

O jertfă lui Zamolxe?

GHEBOSUL

(batjocoritor)

Noului Nemuritor al vostru de pe drumuri adunat?

Cînd se tîra pe-aicea sărîntoc—

Voia să vă omoare zeii...să-şi croiască   25

Opinci din pielea lor. Şi-acum? Acum

îi ridicaţi şi lui jertfelnice!

Ciudat!

Dar ce mai flecăresc? E bine-aşa: de-acum aveţi

Un zeu care-nţelege şi limba voastră.   30

(Ironic.)

Ceilalţi nu vorbesc decît greceşte.

AL DOILEA CULEGĂTOR

Ascuţită limbă ai!

GHEBOSUL

(răutăcios)

Nu pot fi altfel dacă maica-a fost atît de bună

Că mi-a dăruit un spate gras cît pentru trei

Şi-un trup nici pentru unul.   35

Să-mi pun însă zăvor pe gură şi să nu cîrtesc:

Fiecare cu soarta lui. Eu mi-o port

Ascunsă în cocoaşă,

(arătînd spre Ciobanul care se apropie:)

Iar alţii-n lună...Ha-u, ha-u, ha-u.

FIRST HARVESTER

From this much plenty you don't bring

an offering to Zalmoxis?

HUNCHBACK

(*mockingly*)

This New Immortal of yours from roads collected?

When he was crawling around like a mendicant—

he wanted to kill your gods...to cut his slippers   25

from their skin. And now? Now

you offer him sacrifices.

Strange times!

Yet why do they still chatter? It is alright like this: from now on you

Have a god who finally understands your language.   30

(*ironically*)

The others, after all, speak only Greek.

SECOND HARVESTER

A sharp tongue have you.

THE HUNCHBACK

(*mean-spirited*)

I cannot be otherwise since my mother was kind enough

to give me a back thick enough for three

and not enough of a body for one.   35

But let me put a lock on my mouth and not grumble:

each man with his own fate. Mine I carry

hidden in my hump,

(*Gesturing toward the approaching shepherd*)

while the fate of others' is hidden in the moon....ha-u, ha-u, ha-u.

94

Doris C. Plantus

(dispare spre stînga)

CIOBANUL

(păşeşte ca o nălucă)

Că văd ce nimenea nu vede—nu-s de vină.   40

Oamenii m-ascultă cu credinţă fiindcă eu sunt—altul.

Deasupra mea pluteşte luna.

O ating cu degetele dacă vreau.

Sub unghii am lumină din lumina ei.

Eu văd prin ea şi ştiu că-n dosul lumei e Zamolxe.   45

Eu sunt mîna lui.

Un semn,

Şi după mine vine tot norodul.

ÎNTÎIUL CULEGĂTOR

(către Cioban)

Tu eşti sfînt.

AL DOILEA CULEGĂTOR

(sfios, către acelaşi)

De cînd ne-ai coborît din visuri   50

Vestea lui Zamolxe zeul,

E linişte-n cetate.

AL TREILEA CULEGĂTOR

(tot către Cioban)

Ai împăcat pe Mag cu noii mucenici

Şi nu mai curge sînge de prisos.

Zalmoxis

Hunchback exits stage left.

THE SHEPHERD

(stepping like a ghost)

For I see what no one else sees—I am not to blame. 40

People listen to me with faith because I am— another.

Over me floats the moon.

I touch her with my fingertips if I want.

Under my nails I have light of her light.

I see through her, I know on the other side of the moon is Zalmoxis. 45

I am his hand.

A sign,

and after me comes a nation.

FIRST HARVESTER

(to the Shepherd)

 You are a saint.

SECOND HARVESTER

(to the Shepherd)

Since you brought forth from dreams 50

the tale of Zalmoxis the god,

there is peace in the fortress.

THIRD HARVESTER

(also to the Shepherd)

You have reconciled Magus with us the new disciples

and blood no longer runs in excess.

CIOBANUL

Aştept să vie preotesele.   55

Apoi vom merge împreună.

Veniţi şi voi?

CULEGĂTORII

Venim!

CIOBANUL

Şi pentru mine faceţi orişice?

ÎNTÎIUL CULEGĂTOR

(cade la pămînt)

Pentru trimisul lui Zamolxe—orşice!   60

Zi: „umple-ţi părul cu răşină"—

Şi dacă trebuie, îmi voi aprinde părul

Ca să ai o faclă-n miez de noapte.

Zi: „azvîrle-te în sorb",

Şi dacă trebuie eu ma jertfesc—   65

Ca o gutuie coaptă

Ce cade în noroi.

Zi: „aruncă-te în ţeapă",

Şi mîine fi voi ciugulit de paseri ca un strugure.

CIOBANUL

Vreau doar atît,   70

Cînd eu zic da, să ziceţi şi voi da,

Cînd eu zic nu, să ziceţi şi voi nu.

THE SHEPHERD

I am waiting for the priestesses to come.   55

Thereafter we will go together.

Are you coming also?

HARVESTERS

We are coming!

THE SHEPHERD

And you will do anything I say?

FIRST HARVESTER

(falling to the ground)

For the one sent by Zalmoxis—anything!   60

Say to me: "Drench your hair with sap"—

and if necessary, I will set my hair on fire

so that you would have a torch in the middle of the night.

Say: "throw yourself into the bramble"

and if need be I will sacrifice myself—   65

 like a ripe quince

that falls in the mud.

Say: "hurl yourself onto a pike,"

and by this time tomorrow I will be pecked by the birds like a grape.

THE SHEPHERD

I want only this much,   70

that when I say yes, you should also say yes,

when I say no, you should also say no.

Doris C. Plantus

AL DOILEA CULEGĂTOR

Tu eşti sfînt.

AL TREILEA CULEGĂTOR

Tu eşti sfînt.

(Cei trei culegători se duc în vii. Ciobanul se aşază pe un dîlm şi începe să cînte din fluier o doină sfîşietoare. Din pădure sar trei copii, fiecare cu cîte-un fir de trestie în mînă. Se aruncă asupra unui vas cu must şi sug cu trestia.)

CEL MAI MIC

(supărat)

Prin trestia mea nu trece mustul. 75

CEL MAI MARE

E-un pai cu noduri. Du-te smulge-ţi altul—
Găseşti destule-n baltă.

CEL MAI MIC

(începe să plîngă)

Mi-e frică de lipitori.

CEL MAI MARE

(aspru)

Taci. Uite Ciobanul. Vine să te ia.

CEL MIJLOCIU

E ciobanul care se face noaptea priculici. 80

SECOND HARVESTER

You are a saint.

THIRD HARVESTER

You are a saint.

The three harvesters go into the vineyard. The Shepherd sits on a bluff and begins to play a moving ode on the wooden flute. Three children enter from the forest, each one with a reed in hand. They foist themselves over the amphora and suck the fermenting wine through the reeds.

YOUNGEST CHILD

(Upset)

The juice is not coming through my reed.   75

OLDEST CHILD

There is a knot in your straw. Go and pick another—
you'll find plenty in the marsh.

YOUNGEST CHILD

(beginning to cry)

I am afraid of the leeches.

OLDEST CHILD

(annoyed)

Quiet! Look there, the Shepherd! He's coming to take you away.

MIDDLE CHILD

It's the shepherd who turns into a werewolf at night.   80

Doris C. Plantus

CEL MAI MIC

(*ţipă speriat*)

Unde-i?

CEL MAI MARE

(*îl linişteşte*)

Linişteşte-te. Nusitatu, copil neastîmpărat.
Închide ochii—ca să nu te vadă.
Aşa, închide-i bine—
c-apoi se face întuneric   85
şi nu te mai zăreşte nimeni.
I-ai inchis?
Acum e noapte. Nu te văd.
Stai linişit, Nusitatu.

CEL MIJLOCIU

(*şiret, stăpînîndu-şi rîsul*)

Nici eu nu te mai văd.   90

CEL MAI MARE

Nici priculiciul.

(*Cei doi mai mărişori sug iaraşi cu trestiile, iar cel mic—şezînd în iarbă—
strînge din ochi, să-l nu vadă Priculiciul. S-aud rîsete şi chiote, cari s-
apropie. Ciobanul se ridică şi ascultă.*)

UN CULEGĂTOR

(*sare din vie şi ia copii de mînă*)

Ascundeţi-vă! Repede, copii. Să nu vedeţi bacante!
O singură privire de v-atinge, rămîneţi pitici.

YOUNGEST CHILD

(*yells with fright*)

Where is he?

OLDEST CHILD

(*consoling him*)

Calm yourself, Nusitatu, you restless little boy.

Close your eyes— so he can't see you.

That's it, close them tight—

so everything becomes dark   85

and no one can even catch a glimpse of you.

Did you close them?

Now it's night. They can't see you.

Be calm, Nusitatu.

MIDDLE CHILD

(*holding back his laughter*)

Not even I can see you.   90

OLDEST CHILD

Not even the werewolf.

The two older boys resume their drinking through the reeds while the youngest one sits apart on the grass. He is squeezing his eyes shut. Laughter and yelling is heard as someone approaches. The Shepherd stands up and listens.

A HARVESTER

(*jumping out from the grapevines and grabs the children by the hands*)

Hide yourselves! Quickly, children. Beware the Bacchante!

One look from them, and you will remain forever dwarves.

Doris C. Plantus

(se ascund în vie.)

(O ceată de bacante vine din stînga, sălbatic jucînd în livadă. Feţele

verzii. Pletele în vînt. Cîteva bacante învîrtesc şerpi deasupra capetelor,

ca nişte bice. Altele suflă în coarne de bouri. Chiote. Joc. Ciobanul în

mijlocul lor. Culegători curg din vii. Ca la un semn nebunia conteneşte,

apoi dintr-o dată—şi în cea mai mare linişte.)

O BACANTĂ

(îmbrăcată în alb, împrăştie cu mîna cenuşă dintr-o urnă)

Din urnă împrăştiu

Cenuşă de morţi pe cărări—   95

Vîntul s-o piardă spre mări.

Cenuşa celor ce nu mai sînt

O presar pe pămînt

În calea voastră,

Copii, cari încă nu v-aţi născut.   100

Din coarne de zimbri—éha—

Vă chemăm,

Coborîţi-vă toţi cei de mîine,

Voi prunci, luaţi-vă soarta de lut!

Ugerii lumii sunt plini,   105

Prindeţi-i, stoarceţi-i!

Spre azi, nenăscuţilor, curgeţi spre azi!

Miros de moarte adie din brazi,

Lapteze-vă soarele—Treceţi prin scrum,

Strugurii-s copţi, Şi pămîntul întreabă: 110

Sunteţi pe drum? É-ha! E-ho!

Zalmoxis

(The children hide themselves among the vines.)

(A throng of Bacchante enter stage left, dancing wildly in the orchard. Their faces are green. Their tresses in the wind. Some of the Bachante swirl snakes over their heads like whips. Others blow into oxen horns. They make whooping sounds, they dance. The Shepherd is in the middle. The harvesters pour out of the vines. As if by a sign ,the madness ceases all of a sudden. In the greatest of silence-)

BACCHANTE IN WHITE

(dressed in white scatters ashes from an urn.)

From this urn I spread

the ashes of the dead on the roads—   95

let the wind lose them toward the seas.

The ashes of those who are no more

I now sprinkle upon the earth

in your path,

children, who have not yet be born.   100

From the oxen horns—eha—

we call you

to descend all of you of tomorrow,

you infants, take up your fate of clay!

The udders of the world are full,   105

catch them, wring them

toward today, you the unborn, flow toward today!

A smell of death breezes in from through the pines,

the sun suckles you—pass through the ashes,

for the grapes are ripe and the ground asks: 110

are you on your way? E-ha! E-ho!

(din vii răspund sute de guri.)

É-ha! E-ho!

(Jocul bacantelor reîncepe. Strigăte neînţelese. Chiote: éhove, éhove,

éhove! Culegătorii răspund: éhove, éhove, éhove!)

CIOBANUL

(ţine isonul jocului)

Nouă preotese verzi

Sar prin codri şi livezi.

Trec răzoarele cu spini,   115

Sînge curge prin ciulini.

Flutură cu şerpi în vînt,

Peste stele şi pămînt.

Ele nu cunosc cărări,

Ar juca şi-n fund de mări.   120

Ducă-se ca un fior

După dumnezeii lor.

Nebunească-n văi cu chiu,

Tot ce-i mort şi tot ce-i viu.

UN GLAS

Mărire lui Zamolxe!   125

Zalmoxis

Many voices answer back from the vines.

E-ha! E-ho!

The dance of the bacchante begins again. Unintelligble yelling,

whooping: Ehove, ehove, ehove! The harvesters answer back: Ehove,

ehove, ehove!

SHEPHERD

(keeping the dance's beat)

Nine jumping priestesses green

Through forest and orchard seen

Pass through brambled flower beds,   115

Blood through thistle runs blood red

Unfurled on the wind, their snakes in tow,

Over the stars and on the earth below.

To any path they need not keep,

They would dance as much in ocean deep   120

They go like a mad shiver

To follow their gods thither.

They go mad in the valleys shrieking,

At all that is dead and all that is living.

A VOICE

Glory be to Zalmoxis!   125

Doris C. Plantus

BACANTELE

Mărire zeului Zamolxe!

CULEGĂTORII

(din sute de piepturi)

Mărire!

(Strugurii cad aruncaţi din vii în jocul bacantelor. Munţii răspund cu

ecouri.)

CIOBANUL

Să mergem la Marele Mag!

O BACANTĂ

Împlinirea visului s-o cerem!

CIOBANUL

Lăsaţi culesul-n grija ciorilor!   130

Veniţi, jucaţi!

Ehové, Zamolxe!

(Toţi aleargă spre pădure după el☺

Ehové, ehové!

II

Într-o peşteră, gura ei se întrezăreşte în fund. Noapte. Totul se pretrece

ca într-o lume de năluci, cu o ciudată încetineală a vorbei.

ZAMOLXE

(ascuns în întuneric)

M-am coborît tot mai adînc în suflet.

Unde sunt? Unde sunt?   135

Zalmoxis

Glory be to the god Zalmoxis!

HARVESTERS

(from a hundred chests)

Glory!

(Grapes fall from the vines from the dancing. The mountains answer in
echoes.)

SHEPHERD

Let us go to the great Magus!

A BACCHANTE

Let us ask for the fulfillment of the dream.

SHEPHERD

Leave the harvest in the care of the ravens.   130

Come, dance!

Ehové, Zalmoxis!

(All run towards the woods after him)

Ehové, ehové!

II

The inside of a cave, the back is glimpsed through the mouth.
Everything takes place as in a world of ghosts and spirits, with a
strange slowness of speech.

ZALMOXIS

(hidden in the darkness)

I have descended deeper and deeper still into my soul.

Where am I, where am I?   135

ZAMOLXE (CONT)

Tot în peşteră?

Inima vrea să-mi sară din piept—

Văd prin munţi:

Cetatea nu se mişcă ţi totuşi ne apropiem

De-acum.   140

(încet, ca şi cum ar învoca nişte duhuri:)

O frunză cade- noapte,

Un veac se scurge în mine.

Altă frunză cade-n noapte,

Alt veac trece-n mine.

O vedenie se lămureşte într-un colţ al peşterii. Un moşneag care ţine în mînă o cupă. Lumina se răsfrînge de pe arătare în toată peşteră- Zamolxe se ridică şi sprijinindu-se de perete se apropie de nălucă.

ZAMOLXE

Moşneagule, vrei să-ţi şoptesc tot chinul meu?   145

S-ar crede că trăieşti,

Dar ochii nu-i clipesc.

De unde vii?

MOŞNEAGUL

De unde nu e timp.

ZAMOLXE

De-acolo vin numai visurile.   150

MOŞNEAGUL

Şi marii visători.

ZALMOXIS (CONT'D)

Still in the cave?

My heart wants to jump out of my chest—

I can see through the mountains:

the fortress doesn't move and yet we get closer

from now on.   140

(*softly, as if an invocation*)

A leaf falls in the night,

a lifetime drains in me.

Another leaf falls in the night,

another lifetime passes in me.

*An apparition appears in the corner of the cave. An old man holds a cup
in his hand. The light is reflected off the image through the whole cave.
Zalmoxis rises and steadies himself against the cave wall, approaching
the apparition.*

ZALMOXIS (CONT'D)

Old man, shall I whisper to you all my anguish?   145

One would think you live,

but your eyes blink not.

Where have you come from?

OLD MAN

From a place without time.

ZALMOXIS

Only dreams come from that place.   150

OLD MAN

And the great dreamers.

ZAMOLXE

Ce poţi sa-mi spui?

MOŞNEAGUL

Cînd eşti izvor, nu poţi decît să curgi spre mare!

Tu Zamolxe, tu de ce adăşti?

ZAMOLXE

Mi-e teamă că voi duce prea devreme   155

Nouă credinţă între oameni.

MOŞNEAGUL

Prea devreme! Niciodată.

Azi ori mai tîrziu

Te-ntîmpină acelaşi dar!

Viaţa n-are stele pentru noi—   160

Cucuta creşte pe gunoi.

Ce crezi—în cinstea cui?

(Duce cupa la gură, dar se opreşte dintr-odată, apoi urmează cu amară

ironie.)

Era să uit. Cînd ţii ospăţi cu soarta,

Cuvine-se să dai şi zeilor din orice băutură.

De astă dată ţin la datină de a-nchina cu ei.   165

(varsă pe pămînt din băutură)

Beţi şi voi, zei, luminoşi ca putregaiul!

Beţi! Must verde de cucută.

O cupă mi-e prea mult.

(Bea ce rămîne)

ZAMOLXE

Aşa aş închina şi eu cu ei!

ZALMOXIS

What can you tell me?

OLD MAN

When you are a wellspring, all you can do is run to the sea!

You, Zalmoxis, why do you linger in this cave?

ZALMOXIS

I fear that too soon will I bring   155

a new faith among men.

OLD MAN

Too soon! Never.

Today or later

the same gift greets you!

Life has no stars for us—   160

hemlock grows on a dung heap.

What do you think—in whose honor?

(*brings the cup to his mouth, stops at once and then finishes with bitter*

irony.)

I've almost forgotten. When you host destiny,

 it behooves you to give any drink to the gods.

This time I will observe the custom of worshipping with them.   165

(*He spills some of his drink on the ground*)

Drink ye too, gods, bright as rot!

Drink! Hemlock green with fermentation.

A cup is too much for me.

(*He drinks what is left*)

ZALMOXIS

And so would I toast to them as well.

ZAMOLXE (CONT)

Ce vină ispășești? 170

MOȘNEAGUL

Una singură: n-am stat niciodată la-ndoială.

(*se stinge și dispare.*)

ZAMOLXE

(*singur*)

Amare taine-am dezghiocat prin anii mei

Cărunți de-nțelepciune!

Dar nici un trecător nu mi-a ieșit în drum

Să-i altoiesc în inimă răspunsul meu. 175

Cînd zilele răsar pe piscuri,

Părul mi-e de flăcări—

Dar nu e nimeni, nimeni să mă vadă

Trăsnet încremenit pe stînci.

(*încet și rar:*)

O frunză cade-n noapte, 180

Un veac se scurge în mine.

Altă frunză cade-n noapte,

Alt veac trece în mine.

(*Apare un tînăr cu plete lungi și coroană de spini pe frunte. Zamolxe se*

apropie de el.)

Răspunde! Ești soarta mea?

TÎNĂRUL

O nu, dar un prieten tot atît de bun. 185

Ți-aduc un zvon de dincolo.

113

ZALMOXIS (CONT'D)

What blame makes you contrite?   170

OLD MAN

Only one. I never doubted.

(*he grows dark and vanishes*)

ZALMOXIS

(*alone*)

Bitter secrets have I peeled open throughout my years

whitened with wisdom!

But not one traveler crossed my path

that I might graft my answer upon his heart.   175

When the days on peaks arise,

my hair is as flames—

but no one is there, no one to see me

a bolt of lightning frozen upon the rocks.

(*slowly, softly*)

A leaf falls in the night,   180

A lifetime drains in me

Another leaf falls in the night,

Another lifetime passes in me

A young man with long tresses and a crown of thorns on his forehead

appears. Zalmoxis draws near to him.

Answer me! Are you my destiny?

YOUNG MAN

Oh, no, but just as good a friend.

I bring you news from the other side.   185

114

TÎNĂRUL (CONT)

Apropie-se clipa ta, om nou:

În noaptea asta se coc toate smochinele.

Copiii le aşteaptă.

ZAMOLXE

Tu vii ca să le scuturi? 190

TÎNĂRUL

Cad singure, n-auzi?

ZAMOLXE

Aud, mă cheamă cineva în lume.

Simt adieri ca dintr-o mare moartă.

Dar ce vrei cu coroana ta de spini?

TÎNĂRUL

(şi-a luat coroana de pe frunte, îi rupe ghimpii şi-i împrăştie cu gesturi

de semănător)

Seamăn ghimpi sub Calea laptelui 195

Şi-aştept să răsară dureri, multe dureri!

(piere)

ZAMOLXE

(singur)

Cerc în zădar să te mai prind, neînţeleasă arătare.

Te pierzi şi-mi laşi mustrările să le frămînt cu pumnii.

Peşteră, peşteră!

Mi-ai îmblînzit iernile şi mi-ai dospit trecutul 200

YOUNG MAN (CONT'D)

Your moment draws near, new man:

all the figs ripen in this night.

The children wait for them.

ZALMOXIS

Have you come to shake them free? 190

YOUNG MAN

They fall on their own, don't you hear?

ZALMOXIS

I hear. Someone calls me to the world.

I feel the breezes as if from a great death.

But what do you want with your crown of thorns?

(*He has removed the crown from his brow, breaks the thorns and*

spreads them as if sowing seeds.)

YOUNG MAN

I am planting thorns beneath the Milky Way 195

and waiting for sorrows to grow forth, many sorrows.

(*He disappears.*)

ZALMOXIS

(*alone*)

In vain do I try to catch you again, incomprehensible apparition.

You lose yourself and leave me to knead reprimands with my fists.

Cave, cave!

You have made mild my winters and leavened my past 200

ZAMOLXE (CONT)

Sub ocrotirea ta.

Unde-mi sunt amintirile rănite

Pe care mi le-ai mîngîiat pîn'la uitare?

Dă-mi-le, să fiu din nou răzvrătitul!

M-așteaptă soarta,   205

Nerăbdarea mă sugrumă.

Tremurînd îmi iau viața în mîni

Și plec spre viitor, spre mîine-veşnicul!

Ție—peşteră—nu-ți las decît aceste urme

De călcîie tari, şi dacă vrei un strigat.   210

Un strigat de izbîndă ori de cadere—

Cine ar putea să spună?

Zorile s-aseamănă aşa de mult cu amurgul.

Oameni, Zamolxe, paşnicul, reintră în patimile voastre!

Lume, şarpe şi copac   215

Au năpîrlit sub ochii mei—

Şi-am văzut ce-i cheag în haos—

Şi ce-i sîmbure în orice fruct

Căzut în poală vremii.

Sunt sătul de vis.   220

O, stînci, de mult ce v-am privit

m-am făcut şi eu în stîncă.

Vajnic mă topesc

Şi mă revărs din matca mea, nebun,

Spre şesuri şi spre oameni.   225

(mai liniştit)

117

ZALMOXIS (CONT'D)

beneath your watch.

Where are my wounded memories

that you caressed until they were forgotten.

Give them to me now, that I may be the rebel once again!

Destiny awaits me,   205

impatience strangles me.

Trembling, I take my life in my hands

and leave for the future, toward eternal tomorrow!

To you— cave— I leave you nothing but these tracks

of hard heels, and if you want, a shout as well.   210

A shout of victory or failure—

who can say which?

The dawn so resembles the dusk.

People, Zalmoxis, the peaceful one, reenters into your passions!

World, snake, and tree   215

have molted beneath my eyes—

and I have seen what is the clot in chaos—

and what is the seed in any fruit

fallen into the lap of time.

I've had my fill of dreaming.   220

O, rocks, I have looked at you for so long

that I too have made myself a rock.

Vigorously I melt

and spill forth from my origins, mad,

towards plains and people.   225

(quietly)

ZAMOLXE (CONT)

Năluci apar mai multe azi,

Sunt chinuri care muşcă-n pietre.

Altădată nopţile-mi erau un leagăn de odihnă,

Iar ziua lucrurile dimprejur se prefăceau în mine

Intr-un vis atît de liniştit   230

Că reci şi jilave şopîrlele veneau

Să caute soarele

Pe picioarele mele goale.

(încet şi rar)

O frunză cade-n noapte,

Un veac se scurge în mine.   235

Altă frunză cade-n noapte,

Alte veac trece-n mine.

(Se iveşte un bărbat mai în vîrstă, legat pe un rug. Zamolxe întinde

braţele spre el)

Şi tu vrei sa-mi furi—singurătatea?

CEL DE PE RUG

Nu m-ai chemat?—

Sunt numai un ecou al nopţii tale.   240

ZAMOLXE

E-adevărat? Dacă tu şi eu am genunchea

Pe marginea acelui lac, care se cheam-al morţilor

Şi al acelora cari încă nu-s născuţi,

Şi ne-am privi în lac ca-ntr-o oglindă

Am vedea că suntem unul şi acelaşi? E-adevărat?   245

ZALMOXIS (CONT'D)

Ghosts appear more often these days,

there are travails that bite into rock.

Once the nights were a cradle of rest for me,

while during the day, things remade themselves in me

in a dream so peaceful,   230

that cold and damp, the lizards came

to find the sun at my bare feet.

(softly,slowly)

A leaf falls in the night,

a lifetime drains in me.   235

Another leaf falls in the night,

another lifetime passes in me.

Another apparition appears, an older man tied to a stake[2] Zalmoxis

stretches his arms towards him.

And you want to steal— my loneliness?

MAN ON THE STAKE

Did you not call me? –

I am but the echo of your nights.   240

ZALMOXIS

Is this true? If you and I kneeled

on the banks of that lake, that they call the lake of the dead

and of those who have not yet been born,

 if we looked into the lake as if into a mirror

would we see that we are one and the same? Is this true?   245

---

[2] Giordano Bruno, 1548-1600.

CEL DE PE RUG

De cîte ori te cauţi pe tine,

Mă găseşti pe mine.

ZAMOLXE

Cine te-a ridicat pe rug?

CEL DE PE RUG

Cumpătatul veşnic treaz.

ZAMOLXE

Nu-l ştiu. 250

CEL DE PE RUG

Cumpătatul e cel ce te opreşte

Să istoveşti un gînd.

La drumul jumătate te înlănţuie

Şi-ţi strigă: „Destul, nebunule!"

Căci vezi, un gînd întreg e o năpastă. 255

Ci eu îţi zic:

Năpastă? Fie!

Sus omenire către cer

Sau viermii să te roadă în mormînt!

ZAMOLXE

Şi iata Cumpătatul vine şi-ţi aprindă rugul. 260

(Se vede o mînă cu o faclă dînd foc vreascurilor.)

CEL DE PE RUG

Dar pămîntul aude, iar pămîntul nu uită.

MAN ON THE STAKE

As many times as you seek yourself,

you find me.

ZALMOXIS

Who has lifted you onto the stake?

MAN ON THE STAKE

The ever awake and eternal balancer.

ZALMOXIS

I do not know him. 250

MAN ON THE STAKE

The eternal balancer is he who makes you pause

to exhaust a thought.

He arrests you in the middle of the road and chains you there

And cries out to you "Enough, Fool!"

Because, you see, a complete thought is a calamity. 255

Yet I say to you:

Calamity? So be it.

Rise up, mankind, toward the heavens

or else may the worms gnaw at you in the grave.

ZALMOXIS

And behold, the Balancer comes to set fire to your stake. 260

A hand holding a candle lights the kindling.

MAN ON THE STAKE

But the earth hears you, while the earth never forgets.

(dispare încins în flăcări.)

ZAMOLXE

(singur, zbuciumat)

Mi-s ochii beţi de vedenii mai trainice

Decît aceste stînci pleşuve.

Răspunde, inimă! Fii tare, mîna mea!

O jertfă-ţi cere Orbul. 265

Să sfredelesc pămîntul ca un ochi de mare?

Să-mi sfîşiu trupul pentru turma de flămînzi?

Să iau în spate soarele şi să-l cobor în văi?

Ori şi mai mult?

Să plec a două oară-n ţara care m-a-nşelat? 270

Între oameni?

Peşteră. Te schimb în bucium al plecării mele!

(c-un strigăt)

Vino, Orbule, vino—

Să-ţi durez un vad

Spre viaţa noroadelor! 275

(Iese furtunatic din peşteră. O mare de lumină îl întîmpină.)

III

Miez de noapte. Şes întins. Nici un arbore. Calea laptelui—intens

vizibilă. Nici o colină. Magul şi Cioplitorul grec se plimbă amîndoi cu

paşi bătrîni—oprindu-se din cînd în cînd.

He disappears engulfed in flames.

ZALMOXIS

(alone, agitated)

My eyes are drunk with scenes more lifelike

than these bald rocks.

Answer, heart! Be strong, my hand!

The Blind One asks a sacrifice of you.   265

Should I pierce the earth like an eye of the sea?

Shall I tear my body for a flock starving people?

Should I take the sun on my back and carry it down into the valleys?

Or even more than this?

Or shall I go a second time into the country that deceived me?   270

Among the people?

Cave, I change you into a bugle of my departure.

(with a shout)

Come, Blind One, come—

That I should build you a ford in the river

toward the life of the people.   275

He storms out of the cave. A sea of light attends him.

III

Middle of the night. A plain stretches out. Not one tree. The Milky Way is intensely visible. Not one hill. Magus and the Greek Woodcarver are walking about with old steps, stopping from time to time.

MAGUL

Culegători şi preotese mi-au umplut ograda,

Cerîndu-şi noul idol.

Ai început statuia lui Zamolxe?

CIOPLITORUL

De şapte nopţi cioplesc.

MAGUL

Cum e marmura?   280

CIOPLITORUL

E strâvezie

Ca apa cînd în fundul mării cade cerul.

MAGUL

(arată şesul)

Aici e şesul licăririlor de foc.

Din glii zbucnesc lumini de putregai.

Şi pasul triştilor săracilor   285

Se-ndreaptă spre comori ascunse în pămînt

De regii stinşi ai dacilor.

CIOPLITORUL

(arată spre cer)

Priveşte: Calea laptelui. Nici celor care mor—

Nu poate să le pară mai frumoasă.

MAGUS

The harvesters and the priestesses have filled my courtyard

asking after the new idol.

Have you started the statue of Zalmoxis?

WOODCARVER

I have been carving for seven nights.

MAGUS

How is the marble?   280

WOODCARVER

It is as transparent

as water when the sky falls into the bottom of the sea.

MAGUS

(*showing the plains.*)

Here is the plain of the flickers of fire.

They burst into light from the rotting ground.

And the footfall of the sad poor   285

head toward treasures hidden in the earth

of dead Dacian kings.

WOODCARVER

(*showing the sky*)

Behold: the Milky Way. Not even to those who die

can it seem to burn more beautiful.

Doris C. Plantus

MAGUL

(*ridicînd ochii*)

Ce spun de ea bătrînii dascăli greci,   290

De care zeii însişi vin ca ucenici

Să-nveţe—ce e lumea, ce e gîndul—?

CIOPLITORUL

(*oprindu-se*)

Un mit adus de peste mare zice—

Dacă nu mă-nşel—că drumul soarelui

n-a fost întotdeauna unde-i astazi.   295

Şi Calea laptelui nu e decît

Cărarea lui încrucişa pe cea de-acum,

Ogaşele lăsate pe cristalul bolţii

De soare-atîtea mii de ani în urmă

Că nu-i minte să le poată socoti.   300

MAGUL

(*cu privirea în sus*)

Ogaşa soarelui pe drumul veşniciei.

Mă străbate un fior.

(*se aude un bocet depărtat de femei*)

CIOPLITORUL

Femei plîngînd. O fi murit cineva.

MAGUL

Nu. S-a născut un prunc.

CIOPLITORUL

Pe-aicia se boceşte naşterea şi totuşi—   305

MAGUS

(Lifting his eyes)

What do the old Greek teachers say of her?   290

She, to whom the gods themselves go like disciples

to learn—what the world is, what is thought—?

WOODCARVER

(stopping himself)

A myth brought from across the sea says—

if I don't deceive myself—that the path of the sun

wasn't always where it is today.   295

His path crosses the one that is now

and the Milky Way is nothing more than

torrents left on the crystal vault of Heaven,

from so many thousands of years ago

that there isn't a mind that can number them.   300

MAGUS

Torrents of the sun on the road to eternity.

A thrill pierces me through.

(The distant sound of wailing women.)

WOODCARVER

Weeping women. Someone must have died.

MAGUS

No. A babe has been born.[3]

WOODCARVER

In these parts one wails at the birth of a child and yet—   305

---

[3] Herodotus writes that Thracians wept and lamented the birth of a child.

Doris C. Plantus

CIOPLITORUL (CONT)

eu cunosc atîtea ţări şi pot s-o spun—

nu este-un alt popor să-şi mistuie

viaţa ca al tău, înalte Preot!

Ieri am văzut un joc.

Flăcăi săreau peste o suliţă.   310

Se sprijineau de o prăjină şi zburau

—numai aşa: u-hai- hop !

Cînd unul dintre ei rămase mort

Cu burta spintecată-n ţeapă,

Ceilalţi începură-a rîde-n hohote de stîngăcia lui.   315

Şi totul fu numai un joc.

Vezi—cum un fulger nu e om—

Tot atît de puţin e dacul om.

El nu trăieşte.

El se trăieşte.   320

Putere smulsă din potirul uriaşei firi

El n-are nici iubire pentru sine, nici iubire pentru alţii.

Aici am înţeles ca tot ce este—trebuie să fie.

(prinde de braţ pe Mag.)

Opreşte-te, să nu te-mpiedici.

Haina ţi s-a agăţat în spini.   325

MAGUL

Cuvîntul tău stîrneşte în mine temeri nouă.

CIOPLITORUL

Eşti ispitit să crezi că dacii nu nasc om din om.

WOODCARVER (CONT'D)

129

Zalmoxis

I know so much of other countries and I can say it—

there isn't another people who consume their

life like yours, High Priest!

Yesterday I saw a game.

Young men were jumping over a spear.[4]   310

They supported themselves with a pole and thus they flew

—just like that—u-hai-hop!

When one of them was left dead

with his belly impaled on the spearpoint

the others had begun to burst out laughing at his awkwardness.   315

And yet it had only been a game.

See—see how a lightning bolt is not a man—

that's how little a Dacian is a man.

He doesn't live.

He is lived.   320

His strength is plucked from the grail of giant beings,

he hasn't love for himself, nor love for others.

At last I understand that everything is so— because it must be so.

(he catches Magus by the arm.)

Stop, don't trip. Your cloak has caught on the thorns.   325

MAGUS

Your words stir in me a new dread.

WOODCARVER

You are tempted to think that Dacians are not born of man into man.

---

[4] Herodotus describes the ritual in *Histories*, IV.

CIOPLITORUL (CONT)

Nătura-i plăsmuieşte singură, ea însăşi dintr-o dată

Cum îşi face munţii ori izvoarele.

Adu-ţi aminte de Zamolxe,   230

Acel necunoscut, care-ntr-o zi şi-a coborît din munţi

Uimirea, vijelia şi porunca.

I-ai fost vrăjmaş. Te-nţeleg.

Dar el a fost un dac de baştină.

Cînd sfătuia-n parabole,   235

El nu zicea: „trăieşte pentru alţii" sau „fii om",

Ci „fi izvor", „fi fulger".

Şi oare dumnezeul orb al său e altceva

Decît ăst fel al Firei şi al dacilor—

Sălbatic, chinuit, orb, straniu şi veşnic frămîntat?   240

O, nu. Aicea nu mă simt împrejmuit de oameni,

Ci aşa de mult în mijlocul naturii

Încît mă mir că ei au nu mănunchi de muşchi pe cap

În loc de păr—ca stîncile.

MAGUL

(*viclean*)

Da, mă duce amintirea la Zamolxe păduraticul.   245

Nevinovata turmă l-a răstălmăcit

Că azi nici el nu s-ar cunoaşte.

CIOPLITORUL

O, crede-mă,

Cu inima l-au priceput şi-i sunt aproape.

Dar dacii au închipuire de copii.   250

WOODCARVER (CONT'D)

Nature alone created them, she, herself, suddenly

like she makes her mountains or springs.

Remember Zalmoxis, 230

the unknown one, who brought down from the mountains his

wonder, storm, and law.

You were an enemy to him. I understand you.

But he was a native Dacian.

When he advised through parables, 235

he wasn't saying "live for others" or "be a man",

rather "be a spring", "be lightning".

And maybe this blind god of his is something else

other than this kind of the Being's and that of the Dacians—

wild, tormented, blind, strange, eternally tried? 240

Oh, no. I don't feel surrounded by people,

but rather so in the middle of nature

that I wonder how they haven't tufts of moss on the tops of their heads

instead of hair.—like the rocks.

MAGUS

(slyly)

Yes, the memory takes me back to Zalmoxis, wild man of the wood.245

The blameless flock has so distorted him

that today even he wouldn't recognize himself.

WOODCARVER

O, believe me,

with their hearts they understand him and even now are close to him.

But Dacians have the imaginations of children. 250

MAGUL

Dacă ar trăi cum a rîvnit Zamolxe,

Ei s-ar mistui ca focul.

Copiilor le trebuie vis blînd să-i liniștească—

și lumina să le ție-n frîu pornirea,

zăgaz puterilor ce colcăie-n pămîntul lor   255

prea rodnic în izvoare turburi.

CIOPLITORUL

De-i vorbă despre liniște, îți dau dreptate-nalte Preot.

Da—ce-i liniște?

MAGUL

O întrebare căreia-i răspund prin altă întrebare:

De ce furtună oarbă?   260

CIOPLITORUL

(șovăind)

Nu știu.

MAGUL

Nici eu nu știu.

(cu oareșicare teamă)

Și totuși mă opresc.

Tu ești străin și poate vezi mai bine decît mine.

Mi-e frig. Vino maestre. E tîrziu.   265

CIOPLITORUL

Ai crede că răcoarea coboară-ncet

MAGUS

If they would live like Zalmoxis wished them to,

they would consume themselves like fire.

Children need a gentle dream to calm them—

and light to stop them from bolting, to hold back

forces that swarm in their earth   255

too fertile in troubled wellsprings.

WOODCARVER

If it would be a question of peace, I give you the right, High Priest.

But—why peace?

MAGUS

A question I will answer with another question:

why a blind storm?   260

WOODCARVER

(hesitating)

I don't know.

MAGUS

I don't know either.

(fearful)

And yet I stop myself.

You are strange and perhaps see things better than I.

I am cold. Come, Maestro. It is late.   265

WOODCARVER

You would think the coolness descends slowly

CIOPLITORUL (CONT)

Din Calea laptelui

Ca dintr-un fluviu uriaşi. Cetatea nu-i departe.

(*se duc spre dreaptă*)

Te-ai gîndit vreodată Magule?

Magule, ce-ar fi să se întoarcă într-o zi   270

Zamolxe—omul?

MAGUL

(*hotărît*)

Piere el sau poporul!

CIOPLITORUL

Sau el şi poporul!

WOODCARVER (CONT'D)

From the Milky Way

like a giant river. The fortress is not far.

(*they move stage right.*)

Did you ever once think, Magus?

Magus, what would it be like should Zalmoxis return one day   270

—the man?

MAGUS

(*decisively*)

Either he would perish or the people would.

WOODCARVER

Or he and the people both.

ACTUL AL TREILEA

I

Un deal cu o rîpă de lut roşu şi cu şuviţa unui izvor. În stînga se văd turnurile şi zidurile cetăţii. În dreapta începe pădure de stejar. În faţă o livadă cu iarbă mare şi stînci. Dis-de-dimineaţă. Mult soare.

CIOPLITORUL

(Şade sub un stejar pe o stîncă. Pletele cărunte pe umeri. Plăsmuieşte în lut o mică făptură omenească. Lucrează fluierînd.)

ZEMORA

(Tînără şi sălbatică—ciulini în părul despletit—se furişează din pădure la spatele Cioplitorului şi-l gîdilă în plete cu un fir lung de iarbă.)

CIOPLITORUL

(Ridică fruntea dar nu se întoarce. Ghiceşte.)

Zemora—fiica Magului , sau o lăcustă.

ACT THREE

I

A hill with a precipice of red clay and a curling stream of water from a wellspring. On the left, towers and walls of the fortress. On the right starts an oak forest. In the foreground, an orchard with tall grass and rocks. Early morning. Much sun.

WOODCARVER

(The Woodcarver is sitting on a rock beneath an oak tree. White braids on his shoulders. He is creating a small human likeness out of clay. He is whistling as he works.)

ZEMORA

(young and wild, thistles in her unbraided hair, creeps in from the forest behind the Woodcarver and tickles his braids with a long blade of grass.)

WOODCARVER

(raises his brow, but doesn't turn. He guesses.)

Zemora—the daughter of Magus, or perhaps a locust?

Doris C. Plantus

ZEMORA

Şi una şi alta. Căci Zemora turburătoarea

Iubeşte iarba şi soarele

Viu ca lăcustele,

Şi-ar vrea să aibă picioarele   5

Tot atît de verzi,

Verzi ca lăcustele

Sau ca lintea bălţilor.

CIOPLITORUL

Ştiai că mă găseşti—aici?

ZEMORA

Suind cărarea ţi-am văzut în lut   10

Urmele tălpilor. Aşa în şir.

Credeam întîi că-s urme de...măgar.

(rîde)

Auzi pădurea? Numai eu ştiu cum s-o fac să rîdă.

(Rîde cu hohote.)

Auzi cum rîde? Ca un copil mic

Pe care-l gîdili la buric.   15

CIOPLITORUL

(dă din cap)

Zemora, Zemora!

ZEMORA

Ce plămădeşti în lut?

                              ZEMORA

The one and the other. Because the wild Zemora

loves the grass and the sun

alive like the locust,

and she would want to have legs   5

as green,

green like the locust

or the marsh pod.

                          WOODCARVER

Did you know you would find me—here?

                              ZEMORA

Climbing the path I saw your footprints in the clay.   10

Like so, in a row.

At first I was thinking they are the tracks of a ...donkey.

                         (*she laughs*)

Do you hear the forest? Only I know how

to make it laugh

                       (*laughing heartily*)

Do you hear how it laughs? Like a little kid   15

when you tickle his belly button.

                          WOODCARVER

                          (*nodding*)

Zemora, Zemora!

                              ZEMORA

What are you creating out of clay?

Doris C. Plantus

CIOPLITORUL

Un chip al lui Zamolxe.

ZEMORA

L-am auzit de multe ori pe Zamolxe   20

Din cele ce grăia nu pricepeam prea multe.

Dar ochii lui erau aşa de mari

Că trebuia să mă opresc şi să-l ascult.

Odată-l întîlnii pe-aici pe undeva-n pădure

singur.   25

Se chinuia să prind-un roi de-albine

Ce-atîrna de-o creangă ca un cuib.

Lipea cu ceară fundul unei coşniţe,

Cînd i-am sărit în drum:

Zamolxe tu eşti foarte tînăr   30

Şi eu-s frumoasă, dar să nu te sperii.

Te-nvăţ eu cum se prinde roiul,

Tu să-mi povesteşi despre-nceputul lumii.

În astea te pricepi mai bine.

El a tresărit.   35

Îi luai din mîna coşniţa

Şi am proptit-o într-un par deasupra roiului

Ca o căciulă.

El privea tăcut.

Am afumat apoi albinele   40

Cu iasc-aprinsă-n scăpărări de cremene—

141

Zalmoxis

WOODCARVER

A likeness of Zalmoxis.

ZEMORA

I have heard Zalmoxis speak many times   20

though I didn't understand too much of what he spoke.

But his eyes were so big

that I had to stop and listen to him.

One time I met him somewhere here in the forest

alone.   25

He was struggling to catch a swarm of bees[5]

that hovered over a branch like a nest.

He was sealing the bottom of a straw basket with wax

when I leaped out in front of him.

Zalmoxis you are very young   30

and I am beautiful, but do not be afraid.

I will teach you how to catch the swarm,

you will tell me about the beginning of the world.

You understand this much better.

He stirred.   35

I took the basket from his hand

and I propped it up on a pole over the swarm

like a hat.

He watched quietly.

I smoked the bees   40

with a splinter of wood I lit by flint strikes—

---

[5] See Alexander Fol's *Orphica Magica*. Sofia: University "St. Cl. Ohridski", 2004.

ZEMORA (CONT)

Şi ele-au început să se ascundă-n învelişul de nuiele.

Cînd isprăvii, i-am zis:

Făgăduiala, tinere veşnic păduratic!

El m-a-nvălit cu ochii lui ca nişte peşteri   45

Încărcate de surîs, şi trist şi dulce.

Mi-a şoptit:

O, ţie trebuie să-ţi spun un lucru,

Nu cu mintea să-l pricepi,

Ci cu frumseţea ta sălbatică.   50

Nu ştiu. Visez? Se pare

Ci Orbul a creat femeia în aceeaşi zi

În care a făcut şi—luna.

CIOPLITORUL

Poate din una şi aceeiaşi groaznică lumină.

Fiinţe gememe.   55

ZEMORA

Apoi Zamolxe fugi în codru. Roiul l-a uitat acolo.

Iar la patru zile a urmat

Nenorocirea din livada-aceasta.

CIOPLITORUL

(îi întinde micul chip de lut)

Zemora, spune-mi seamănă cu prinzătorul tău

de roiuri?   60

ZEMORA (CONT)

and they began to hide in the wicker covering.

When I finished, I told him

Promise, eternal young wild man of the wood!

He enfolded me with his eyes like caves   45

filled with smiles, yet sad, and sweet, too.

He whispered to me:

Oh, I must tell you something,

Do not know it with your mind,

but rather with your wild beauty.   50

I don't know. Am I dreaming? It seems

the Blind One has created woman on the same day

that he also created—the moon.

WOODCARVER

Maybe from one and the same awesome light.

Twin beings.   55

ZEMORA

Afterwards Zalmoxis ran into the forest. He forgot the swarm there

while on the fourth day followed

misfortune from this orchard.

WOODCARVER

(he offers her the small clay figurine)

Zemora, tell me, does this resemble your

bee-catcher?   60

Doris C. Plantus

ZEMORA

(privind de aproape chipul)

Zamolxe-a fost prea mult privire,

Iar aceasta-i prea mult om.

(linguşitoare.)

Un dar pentru Zemora? Da?

CIOPLITORUL

(îşi ia chipul)

Nu. E pentr-un altar de casă.

ZEMORA

(supărată)

Pentr-un altar de casă?   65

Al cui?

CIOPLITORUL

Al marelui diregător.

Uitaşi că mîine-i sărbătoarea zeilor necunoscuţi?

(se ridică să plece)

ZEMORA

Vrei să pleci?

CIOPLITORUL

Mă duc spre casă să mai poleiesc   70

Statuia lui Zamolxe, cea de marmură.

Tu încotro?

(ia în braţe un cocoloş de lut)

Zalmoxis

                        ZEMORA
              (looking closely at the figure)
Zalmoxis was too much to behold,

while this is too much man.

                      (flatteringly)
A gift for Zemora? Yes?

                      WOODCARVER
                (taking back the figurine)
No. It is for a house altar.

                        ZEMORA
                        (angry)
For a house altar?   65

Whose?

                      WOODCARVER
The great leader's.

Have you forgotten tomorrow we honor the unknown gods?

                    (he rises to leave)
                        ZEMORA
Do you want to leave?

                      WOODCARVER
I am going home to polish   70

the statue of Zalmoxis some more, the one of marble.

Which way are you headed?

              (he takes a lump of clay in his arms.)

ZEMORA

În sus, să-mi usc sandalele

La soare. Sunt umede de rouă.

CIOPLITORUL

Tot spre soare, tot spre soare? 75

ZEMORA

Tot spre soare şi-n pădure!

(Cioplitorul dispare pe cărăruie în stînga, iar Zemora în pădure.)

(Pauză. Cîntec de paseri.)

ZAMOLXE

(din altă parte a pădurei, soseşte în livadă, luminos. O măciucă în mînă

şi funigei în barbă.)

Livada-n care m-au lovit.

Potecile-acelaşi. Cetate, eşti aici?

Pleoapele-mi se zbat de cerul tău

Ca nişte fluturi de-o fereastră. 80

Nu-i numai poveste? Sunt aici?

(pipăie cu mîna un arbore.)

Cu palma pipăi scoarţa asprului copac

Şi simt că sunt aievea.

Fruct copt m-am rupt din creanga unui dumnezeu

Şi cad aici 85

În pragul tău, cetate!

Unde ţi-e rugul?

M-aştepţi? Mai ai vreun prieten pentru mine?

Unde ţi-s spinii? Cu ce mîni primi-vei soarele,

Ce ţi-l cobor din piscuri 90

ZEMORA

Up there, to dry my sandals

in the sun. They are damp with dew.

WOODCARVER

Still to the sun, ever to the sun?   75

ZEMORA

Ever toward the sun and into the forest!

(*The Woodcarver disappears on a path stage   left, while Zemora, into*

the woods.)

(*A pause. Birdsong.*)

ZALMOXIS

(*In another part of the forest Zalmoxis arrives in the orchard, luminous.*)

The orchard where they struck me.

The paths are the same. Fortress, are you here?

My eyelids struggle against your sky

like butterflies against the window pane.   80

Is it not just an illusion? Am I really here?

(*he touches a tree*)

I feel the sharp bark of the tree

and I can feel that I am actually here.

Like a ripe fruit I broke myself from the branch of a god

and fall here   85

on your threshold, fortress!

Where is your stake?

Do you wait for me? Do you have another friend for me?

Where are your thorns? With what hands will you receive the sun

that I will bring down for you from peaks   90

Doris C. Plantus

ZAMOLXE (CONT)

Darnic în lumină?

Pui de mesteacăni cresc pe ziduri—

Un semn că nu te-ai istovit în lupte mari

De cînd plecai, norod nebun.

Odihnă multă ai avut   95

s-arunc năvoade în noianul veşniciei.

Pescuit-ai frămîntări din ape fără fund?

Poate −i-ai ars de mult toţi zeii.

Năruitu-ţi-ai altarele cu capete de zimbri?

Nădejdea mea e încă tot cu ochii   100

Mari deschişi spre viitor. Cred mult.

Sunt răbduriu.

(Îşi îndreaptă ochii cercetători spre cărare.)

Livada-n care m-au lovit.

Cîinii ciobanilor pribegi au lins

În treacăt sîngele ce mi s-a scurs   105

Pe pietrele cărărilor.

Un semn că astă mă iubeşti—cetate?

Un semn că mîine-o să ridici un templu

Orbului?

Oricum ar fi, nu mă-nspăimînt—   110

Şi greu de viaţă şi de gîndul morţii

Îmi azvîrl destinul între zidurile tale,

Tainică cetate!

Munţii vin cu mine.

(se opreşte şi ascultă. Un cîntec s-aude din stejeriş.)

149

ZAMOLXIS (CONT'D)

generous in light.

Babes of birch grow on the walls—

a sign that you did not exhaust yourself in great battles

since you left, crazy people.

You had plenty of rest   95

to cast your nets in the multitude of eternity.

Did you fish worries from bottomless waters?

Maybe you have burned your gods a long time ago.

Have you crumbled your altars with heads of oxen?

My hope is ever wide-eyed toward the future.   100

I believe many things.

I am patient.

           (He directs his searching gaze toward the path)

The orchard where they struck me.

The stray dogs of shepherds licked

the blood that dripped from me on   105

stony path I crossed.

A sign that today you love me—o fortress?

A sign that tomorrow you will raise a temple

to the Blind One?

How ever it will be, I shall fear not—   110

and heavy with life, and the thought of death

I hurl my destiny into your walls,

secret fortress.

The mountains come with me.

        He stops and listens. A song is heard from the oak forest.

Doris C. Plantus

GLASUL ZEMOREI

Hoinăresc spre soare— 115
Din frunziş răsfrînt
El îmi cade-n harfă.
Nu mai ştiu să cînt.
Zarişte pleşuvă.
Gîndul mi-e nătîng. 120
Alb măceş mă cheamă
   Şi iau drum-n crîng.

Ghimpi se-nfig în mînă.
Şerpi trec prin amurg.
Şi din răni pe strune 125
Stropi de sînge-mi curg.
Coarde prind să cînte
   Screi în urechi.
Picuri cad într-una
   Peste taine vechi. 130

(Zemora reapare în livadă cu un mănunchi de flori.)

ZAMOLXE

(uimit)

Întîiul om. De şapte ani întîiul om
Îmi mîngîie vederea.

(se apropie de Zemora.)

Fecioară, proaspătă ca dimineţile de toamnă,
Ce cîntec spui?

VOICE OF ZEMORA

Turned out from the greenery   115

Toward the sun I wander

He falls so onto my harp[6]

That I can sing no longer.

The horizon is sparse.

My mind is struck dumb.   120

The white rose calls me

From the road to the grove I come.

The thorns dig into my hand,

Snakes through twilight tarry

Drops of blood from my wounds run   125

upon the harp strings I carry .

The strings catch tiny insects

to sing in my ears

Droplets fall together

over ancient secrets.   130

(*Zemora reappears in the orchard with a bunch of flowers*)

ZALMOXIS

The first human. After seven years the first human

Caresses my sight.

(*He draws near to Zemora*)

Maiden, as fresh as autumn mornings,

what song are you saying?

---

[6] Orfeus was a Thracian god.

152

Doris C. Plantus

ZEMORA

Tu eşti străin pe-aici,   135
Ciobanii-l fluieră de mult,
Iar vorbele i le-a scornit Madùra
Cîntăreţul.

ZAMOLXE

Îl cunoscui pe vremuri. Mai trăieşte?
A murit?   140

ZEMORA

Trăaia în cetăţuia lui, tot singur,
Pînă ce-şi ucise sufletul-
Nu ştie nimenea de ce. Oameni spun
Că într-o noapte-au auzit
Copite de-argint pe drum în jos.   145
Asemenea chitarelor sunt drumurile,
Cu cît mai vechi răsună mai frumos.
Şi-apoi în colb de lună
s-a văzut un roib în goană.
Fără de stăpîn în şea   150
Se întorcea splinatic la castel.
Legată cu o funie de coadă
Tîra în urma lui o harfă—ca un mort.

ZAMOLXE

Aşa mor cîntăreţii daci.

ZEMORA

You are a stranger to these parts,   135

for the shepherds have long played it on their flutes,

while the bard, Madura

made up the words.

ZALMOXIS

I used to know him, a long time ago. Is he still alive?

Has he died?   140

ZEMORA

He lived in his little citadel, all alone,

Until he murdered his own soul.

No one knows why. People say

that one night they had heard the sound of

silver hoofbeats on the road below.   145

Likewise guitars are roads,

the older they are, the more beautiful the sound.

And then in moon-dust

an auburn stallion galloped out

without a rider in the saddle   150

 and made back for the castle at breakneck speed.

Tied to his tail a harp

dragged at the end of a rope—like a dead man.

ZALMOXIS

That is how the Dacian bards die.

ZEMORA

(mişcată)

Nu-ţi pare că auzi amarul rîs   155

Al celui care nu mai vrea să se întoarcă în viaţă

Şi-şi trimite calul singur înapoi?

Şi nu vezi roibul biciuit sălbatic

De căderi de stele?—pe drum în jos

Tîrăşte-n urma lui o harfă   160

Ca un mort.

ZAMOLXE

Din partea mea-l pricep aşa de bine

Pe Madùra.

(dintr-o dată stăruitor:)

Îmi mai îngădui-o întrebare?

Florile, pentru cine sunt florile?   165

ZEMORA

Le duc la templu. Opreşte-te şi tu-n cetate

Pentr-o zi, străinule. E sărbătoare-n zori.

Poporul o s-aşeze-n sanctuar

Statuia lui Zamolxe.

Eu îi mai jertfesc şi miere.   170

Cînd a fost pe-aici l-am învăţat

Să prindă roiuri.

(pleacă cu un surîs.)

ZAMOLXE

(rămîne împietrit, cu ochi turburi îndreptaţi spre cetate.)

ZEMORA

(*affected*)

Are you not saddened by the bitter laughter   155

of one who no longer wants to return to life

and sends his horse back alone?

And do you not see the auburn horse whipped into a frenzy

by falling stars? —on the road below

a harp drags behind him   160

like a corpse.

ZALMOXIS

For my part, all too well do I know

Madura.

(*suddenly emphatic*)

Will you grant me another question?

The flowers—for whom are the flowers?   165

ZEMORA

I am taking them to the temple. You should stop and rest in the fortress

for a day, stranger. At dawn begins a holiday.

The people will dedicate a statue of the

god Zalmoxis in the sanctuary.

I will make an offering of honey in his name.   170

When he was among us, I taught him

how to catch swarms of bees.

(*Zemora leaves smiling.*)

ZALMOXIS

Zalmoxis remains dumbfounded, staring with troubled eyes toward the

fortress.

II

O uliţă în cetate. Noapte. Lună.

ZAMOLXE

(trece cu capul aplecat)

Cîntă cocoşii de munte.

Prietenii unde-mi sunt?

Nu-i mai găsesc.   175

Troscoţel a crescut prin ograzile lor

Şi iarbă pe vetrele lor.

Nu mai bate inimă!

Căderi pe ape s-aud din vale,

Ori poate-s adieri din rîul morţilor.   180

Iată şi umbra mea—

n-am înţeles-o niciodată.

Eu o arunc şi totuşi e mai mare decît mine.

Adieri din rîul morţilor.

Şi iaraşi cîntă cocoşii de munte.   185

Inimă,

Taci!

(Dispare. Pe urma lui se furişează Ghebosul, iscodind.)

II

An alleyway behind the fortress. Night. The moon is shining.

ZALMOXIS

(*passes with his head bowed.*)

The mountain birds are singing.

Where are my friends?

I will not find them.   175

Bramble has overgrown their orchards

and grass now covers their hearths.

Beat no more, Heart!

You can hear the rush of waterfall in the valley,

or perhaps it is only the breeze of the river of the dead.   180

And here is my shadow, too—

I have never understood it.

I cast it from me and still it is greater than I am.

Breezes from the river of the dead.

And once more sing the mountain birds.   185

Heart,

be silent.

(*He disappears. The hunchback trails quickly behind him.*)

III

În templu. Un perete lateral al templului formează fondul. Altarul, nevăzut, în stînga; în formă de potcoavă sunt aşezate piedestale cu statuile celor şase zei principali; unul dintre aceştia, mai mare, are cap de bour. În mijlocul potcoavei altarul de jertfă. Un piedestal e liber fără statuie. Mai spre dreapta, două columne puternice de culoare arămie sprijinesc bolta. Intrarea în templu e în dreapta, dar nu se vede. Jertfelnice şi un şir întreg de zei mărunţi lîngă peretele din fund. Lumină vagă se răsfrînge de sus. Flăcări ard pe altar şi-n jertfelnice. Templul e gol.

ZAMOLXE

(Intră singur din dreapta. Ochi aprinşi. Se opreşte lîngă columna din faţă.S-aud strigăte depărtate.)

Mulţimea-i adunată-ntru slăvirea mea.

Pe lîngă ea trecui şi m-a privit cu ochi streini.

Oamenii uită. Nimenea nu mă mai ştie.   190

Răcnetele lor de bucurie-ar vrea

Să mă ridice-n cer,

Dar fără-nvăţătura mea.

Miros de vin mă abureşte.

Ce reci sunt lespezile!   195

MAGUL

(A ieşit din altar în odăjdii de in alb şi, punînd tămîie în jertfelnice, vede pe strein.)

Streinule, ai îndrăznit?

Nu ţi-a fost frică să treci pragul

Înainte de-a intra statuia lui Zamolxe?

III

In the temple. A lateral wall represents the background. The six principal gods are arranged in a horseshoe on pedestals. One is larger than the rest, and has the head of a bull. The sacrificial altar is in the center. One pedestal is empty. Two tall brass-colored pillars support the vault. The temple entrance is to the right but unseen. Sacrifices in rows of small graven images are along the back wall. A vague light reflects from above. Candles burn on the altar.

The temple is empty.

ZALMOXIS

(Zalmoxis enters stage right. His eyes are bright. He stops next to the column upstage. In the distance the sound of yelling.)

The masses are gathered in my glory.

I walked past them and they looked at me with strange eyes.

People forget. No one remembers me anymore.   190

Their joyful clatter would

lift me to the heavens,

but without my teaching.

The smell of wine sprays me.

How cold are these tombstones.   195

MAGUS

(Magus comes out of the altar in white vestments and notices the stranger, while putting incense on the altar table.)

You there, Stranger! How dare you?

Did you not fear to cross this threshold

before the statue of Zalmoxis enters?

MAGUL (CONT)

Nimănui dintre profani   200

Nu i se-ngăduie ăst pas.

ZAMOLXE

(tace)

MAGUL

(s-apropie, îi ţinteşte cu privirea şi parcă şi-ar aduce aminte.)

O, norii turburi ai acestor ochi.

Aşa schimbat? Aici? Din nou aici?

Şi tocmai azi?

Zamolxe, te cunosc.   205

(ca sugrumat.)

De ce te-ai întors? De ce te-ai întors?

Poporul se răzbună

Fără să vrea, fără să ştie.

(cu un rîs rău.)

Ai încercat să-l scapi de zei

Şi azi îţi ai şi tu   210

Un chip de piatră printre ei!

ZAMOLXE

(cu un hohot)

Şi tu, tu eşti preotul meu!

Ha—ha, de necrezut! Ce răzbunare blestemată!

MAGUL

Aşa de tînăr tu ai sămînţat un gînd

Şi rodul nu l-ai aşteptat. E greu sa-l schimbi.   215

MAGUS (CONT'D)

No one among the profane   200

would take such steps.

ZALMOXIS

(*silent.*)

MAGUS

(*Magus draws near, eyes him and reacts as though he remembers.*)

O, the troubled gaze of these eyes.

So changed? Here? Here again?

And today of all days?

Zalmoxis, I know you.   205

(*choking as though strangled*)

But why have you returned? Why have you come back?

The people are rioting

without wanting, without knowing why.

(*with mean laughter*)

You tried to wean them from statues,

 and today, you too will have   210

a stone carved in your image among them!

ZALMOXIS

(*laughing*)

And you, you are my priest!

Ha—ha, unbelievable! What an accursed rebellion!

MAGUS

So young were you when you sowed a thought

and expected not such a fruit to flower. It is difficult to change.   215

Doris C. Plantus

MAGUL (CONT)

Dintr-un ogor răsare ceea ce sameni,

Dar din inimi nu.

Aci pui grîu şi cresc cireşi.

(*linguşitor*)

De altfel nu te bucuri?

Toate aceste arămii columne   220

Ca nişte fecioare zvelte ce şi-au aruncat veşmîntul

Joacă-n jurul tău.

Ai un altar şi-o lume-ţi cade-n pulbere.

(*aspru*)

Pleacă înapoi! Altarul n-are trepte!

Eşti sus—zadarnic cerci—nu poţi   225

Să-l mai cobori.

Răzvrătire?

Împotriva cui?

Azi nu mai ai nici un vrăjmaş,

Poporul ţi se-nchină—   230

Şi eu-preotul tău!

ZAMOLXE

Tu eşti preotul meu!

Ha-ha! Dar n-o să plec.

Mă-mplînt aici în lespezi.

Fulgere, cu pumnii încleştaţi vă strîng!   235

MAGUL

O, dumnezeul tău e orb—

Şi tu biet tînăr i-ai luat pe umeri soarta.

MAGUS (CONT'D)

You surely reap what you sow from a field,

but from a human heart, no.

Here you plant wheat, and cherries grow.

(flatteringly)

Otherwise, are you not pleased?

All of these bronze-colored columns   220

stand like slender young maids who have cast off their robes

dancing all around you.

An altar have you and people to fall on their knees in the dust for you.

(bitterly)

Go back! The altar has no steps!

You are high above us—but in vain you search—you can never   225

take him down.

Rebellion?

Against whom?

Today you have no enemies left,

the people worship you—   230

and I, I am your priest!

ZALMOXIS

You are my priest!

Ha-ha! But I will not leave this place.

I will hurl myself upon these stone slabs.

Lightning, with my clenched fist will I squeeze you!   235

MAGUS

O, your god is blind—

and you, poor youth have taken fate upon your shoulders.

ZAMOLXE

Şi soarta-aceasta mă face să lovesc.

MAGUL

Norodul nu va crede că eşti tu.

Loveşti? Pe cine? Ai vreun duşman?   240

Doar vremea, vremea—care-a aşezat

Piatră cu piatră, şi ţi-a ridicat

Un templu!

Trăsneşte-o!

ZAMOLXE

C-un bici de fulger   245

Voi întoarce vremea înapoi—

Şi mîine va fi ieri!

Dintr-un adînc striga-voi de pe ţărmul meu stingher,

Şi vremea se va trage înapoi

Ca marea cînd o cheamă luna.   250

Şi-atunci m-apropiu de urechea ta

Şi-ţi zic:

Grăbeşte-te—

Îngroapă-ţi zeii cioclule bătrîn!

E plin hoituri de cerul tău!   255

MAGUL

Eşti tînăr şi orb.

    A doua oară vii. De ce?

N-ai fost în stare să rămîi,

De ce te-ai mai întors?

Du-te, pleacă!   260

ZALMOXIS

And this fate makes me strike out.

MAGUS

The people will not believe it is you.

You strike out? At whom? Have you an enemy?   240

Only time, time—who has set

stone upon stone and raised

a temple for you!

Strike it!

ZALMOXIS

With a whip of lightning   245

Will I turn back time and after—

tomorrow too will be today!

From the deep I will call out from my lonesome shore

and time will turn back

like the sea when the moon beckons it.   250

And then I will draw close to your ear and

tell you:

make haste—

bury your gods, old undertaker!

Your sky is full of rotting corpses!   255

MAGUS

You are young, and blind.

    You come back a second time. Why?

You chose not to remain among us,

so why have you returned?

Go away, leave us!   260

MAGUL (CONT)

Ori nu.

Ţi-e foame?

Ai avut ce să mănînci

În ascunzişul tău atîţia ani?

Ce chinuri. Mă topesc de mila ta. Eşti slab.   265

Du-te! Dar zilele cînd s-or mici de frig

Şi foamea te va roade,

Îţi îngădui să te-întorci,

Din cînd în cînd,

Necunoscut—ca cerşetor,   270

Să stai aici pe treptele acestor stîlpi

Şi să-ţi întinzi spre trecători

Tremurătoarea mînă.

Se vor găsi şi oameni care să-ţi dea

O pîine şi un strop de vin   275

Din toamna lor răscoaptă.

Rămăşiţile ce prisosesc

De la altarul tău

De asemenea le vei primi din îndurarea mea.

Am lacrime de milă pentru tine.   280

O nu-încerca a doua oară furia norodului.

Eu nu sunt rău, dar pleacă unde ştii!

Ca cerşetor mai poţi să vii—

Aci, pe treptele acestui templu,

Cînd eşti flămînd   285

Şi viscolul se va-ncălzi sub zdreanţa ta!

MAGUS (CONT'D)

Or not.

Are you hungry?

Did you have anything to eat

in your little hideaway all those years?

What sufferings. I melt from pity. You are weak.   265

Go! When the days shrink with cold

and hunger gnaws at you,

you dare to return

from time to time,

unknown—like a beggar,   270

 you should stand on the steps of these columns

and stretch your trembling hand

to those who pass by.

You will find people who will give you

a crust of bread and drop of wine   275

from their overripe harvest.

Likewise, will you receive the remains

left over on your altar by

my mercy.

Tears of pity have I for you.   280

O, do not try the fury of your people a second time.

I am not evil, but you should leave this place.

You can always come back as a beggar—

Here, upon the steps of this temple

when you are hungry   285

and the snowstorm will warm beneath your ragged cloak.

(Zamolxe se clatină şi se sprijineşte de columnă. Zdrobit de strigătele mulţimei care se apropie de templu: „Ehove, ehove, Zamolxe!" Ciobanul şi-un alt dac aduc pe umeri statuia zeului Zamolxe şi-o aşează pe piedestalul gol. Popor mult s-adună. Locul unde e Zamolxe-omul rămîne însă aproape gol. Tot timpul cîntă.)

CORUL COPIILOR

Prin uliţi ţi-am purtat

Cioplitul chip—şi goi

Căzurăm în nisip.

Nu suntem buni şi mici?   290

Şi nu-s sub streşine

    Atîtea rîndunici

Ce şi-au zidit un lut

    Cuibarul scund şi sfînt?

    O nu te turbura!   295

    Şi pentru noi, bieţi prunci,

Zamolxe, zeu lovit,

    Îndură-te, preabun,

De cei ce te-au ţintit

Cu praştii de alun!   300

O nu trăsni pe cei

De faţa ta s-ascund,

Şi iezii mai ales

Să ni-i fereşti pe stînci

De rîpele adînci,   305

Tu groaznic nenţeles!

Zalmoxis

Zalmoxis shakes so with emotion that he must steady himself against the column. He is overcome by the shouts of the multitude that approach the temple; "Ehove, ehove, Zalmoxis!" The Shepherd and another Dacian carry the statue of Zalmoxis on their shoulders and put it down on the empty pedestal. Many people gather, yet where Zalmoxis is standing, there is no one beside him. Constant singing.

CHORUS OF CHILDREN

We carried your carved image

through the streets—and naked

fell on the sand.

Are we not small and good?   290

And are there not beneath the eaves

many swallows

who made their nests of clay,

so shallow and holy?

O, do not disturb them!   295

For our sake, poor children,

Zalmoxis, the god who was struck,

Harden yourself too well

against those who took aim at you

with slingshots made of hazelnut wood.   300

Please, do not condemn those

who hide from your face,

and especially, the kid-goats

should you guard against the steep ridges

deep ravines,   305

You, so awesomely misunderstood!

Doris C. Plantus

MAGUL

(în faţa statuilor)

Din praful ud

De vinul sfînt—

Statuia albă, ridicaţi-o pe altar!

Cădeţi, cădeţi!   310

(Poporul îngenunchează. Magul ridică braţele spre statuia lui Zamolxe.)

Întoarce-te Zamolxe-ntre stăpînii cei dintîi

Ai gîndurilor, brazdelor,

Luminei şi ai apelor!

Răsune stelele-n ecouri

Sub sandalele-nălţării tale.   315

Urcă pragul veşniciei

Îi mîngîie cu mîna ta

Ursita ăstui trist norod.

Cădeţi, cădeţi!

E ziua tuturor părerilor de rău.   320

Nisip aţi aruncat în ochii soarelui.

Iertare!

Plîngeţi să miroase-a lacrimi templul!

Înalţă-te, Zamolxe!

POPORUL

Înalţă-te, înalţă-te, înalţă-te!   325

MAGUL

(pleacă spre altarul nevăzut din stînga)

Ieşiţi, fecioare! Jocul sacru să înceapă!

Zalmoxis

MAGUS

(in front of the statues)

From wet dust

Of holy wine

Raise the white statue upon the altar!

Fall to your knees, fall down!   310

(*The people kneel. Magus raises his arms in supplication to the statue.*)

Turn back, Zalmoxis, from the first masters

of thought, of the furrowed earth,

of light and of the waters!

May the stars resound in echoes

beneath the sandals of your ascent.   315

Raise the threshold of eternity

and caress these sad people

with your prophetic hand.

Kneel, kneel!

It is the day of all sorrows.   320

You have thrown sand in the eyes of the sun.

Forgiveness!

Weep, all of you, so the temple can smell your tears.

Arise, Zalmoxis!

VOICES OF THE PEOPLE

Arise, arise, arise!   325

MAGUS

(moves to the altar unseen.)

Maidens, come all, begin the sacred dance!

172

(Şase fecioare, în frunte cu Zemora, vin în faţa statuilor divine şi se

închină pe rînd fiecare la cîte unul din cei şase zei)

ÎNTÎIA

(în faţa zeului cu cap de bour)

Vîlvele reci

Din mine de aur

Fie-ţi soţii,

Puternice taur.   330

A DOUA

Ochii mi-s dulci,

Am trup de petale,

Fîlfîie în zbor

Cu clipele tale.

A TREIA

Floare şi om   335

În glod ţi să-nchine—

Foc pe altar

Mă mistui în mine.

A PATRA

Luna o-ncarc

Cu bobi de tămîie,   340

Jarul nestins

În ea să-ţi rămîie.

Six maidens led by Zemora come in front of the divine statues. Each one
bows down in turn to each of the six statues.

FIRST MAIDEN

(in front the god with the head of a bull)

May cold ripples from

mines of gold

be your mates,

o, powerful bull.   330

SECOND MAIDEN

My eyes are sweet

I have a body of petals,

they flutter in flight.

with your blinking.

THIRD MAIDEN

Flower and man   335

in mud worship you

fire on the altar

spreads its mist in me.

THE FOURTH MAIDEN

I fill the moon with

nuggets of incense,   340

undying embers

in her remain for you.

A CINCEA

Trîmbe de fum

Se-nalţă spre tine

Inimi şi joc   345

Să-ţi fie vecine!

ZEMORA

(la statuia lui Zamolxe)

Miere-ţi jertfesc

În scrum şi-n jeratic,

Ţie—stupar

Etern păduratic!   350

(Începe jocul fecioarelor însoţit de chitare din altar. În vremea asta:)

ZAMOLXE

(tot lîngă columnă, după ce-a privit tulburat)

Mă-năbuş. Friguri în vîrtej

Îmi scutură din temeile cerul.

Nu-i trupul meu în cer?

Dar stelele, stelele chiar,

Pe altădată le-am iubit,   355

Mi s-ar părea amare azi.

Otravă verde picură din ele-n cupa mea

Ca din strivite capete de şerpi.

Eu—zeu?

Credinţa mea v-a ispitit—altare,   360

Cu mii de jertfitori netoţi!

La luptă pumni!

THE FIFTH MAID

Trumpets of smoke

climb toward you

May hearts and dance   345

always be your neighbors!

ZEMORA

(at the statue of Zalmoxis)

Honey I offer you

in ash and ember,

To you—beekeeper

eternal wild man of the woods!   350

The dance of the maidens begins, joined by guitars from the altar.

Meanwhile:

ZALMOXIS

(still standing beside the column, having watched on with worry.)

I am smothered. Fevers in a whirlpool

shakes me from the foundations of heaven.

Is not my body in the sky?

But the stars, the actual stars,

that I so loved in another time,   355

would seem to me today bitter.

Green poison trickles from them into my cup

as though from the crushed heads of snakes.

I—a god?

My faith has tempted you—altars,   360

With thousands of mindless worshipers!

My fists make ready for battle.

Doris C. Plantus

ZAMOLXE (CONT)

Vrăjmaşul?

Eşti tu—numai tu, numai tu chip de piatră-ncoronat

Cu nemurire 365

Şi dezmierdat cu jocuri de fecioare.

(întinde braţele.)

Zeule Zamolxe, cît eşti de alb zăpadă!

Dar visul meu e cald şi te topesc.

Aici sunt eu

Şi omenescul meu gînd. 370

Acolo? Eu zeul,

Şi toţi beţivii jertfei.

Statuie,

Cu povara ta de munte

Mi te ridici pe piept. 375

Blestem,

Ucigătorule de visuri!

Iată, mă ridic în faţa ta—

Nu tremuri?

Vrăbii îşi vor face cuib în capul tău! 380

Zamolxe-Zeule,

De te-aş vedea în mărăcini

Sau pe gunoi

La lună cînii să te latre!

Cenuşă—vîntul—să te spulbere-n nori. 385

În lături jerfitori—

Şi vreme, înapoi ca marea, înapoi!!

Zalmoxis

The enemy?

It is you—and only you, an image chiseled in stone, crowned

in immortality 365

and doted upon by the dances of maidens.

(*stretching out his arms.*)

Zalmoxis, the god, how white you are like snow!

But my dream is warm and I will melt you.

Here am I

with my human thought. 387

And there? I, the god,

and all the drunkards of sacrifice.

Statue,

with your burden of the mountain

lift me to your bosom. 375

Damnation,

slayer of dreams!

Behold, I rise before you—

do you not tremble?

The swallows will make nests in your head! 380

Zalmoxis, the god,

should I see you in the bramble

or in a dung heap,

may the dogs howl you to the moon!

Ash—the wind—may it scatter you into the mud. 385

your followers beside you—

and time, turn back like the sea, turn back!!

(Se aruncă asupra statuiei sale şi o doboară cu pumnii. Poporul,

îngenuncheat, îl priveşte neînţelegător, se ridică. Tumult. S-aud

strigate: „Statuia" „Zeul", „Spart", „Altarul pîngărit", „O, vai", „Ucideţi-

l!" Vreo cîţiva ciobani se reped asupra lui Zamolxe, îl răstoarnă şi-l

trăsnesc cu bucăţi din statuia spartă. Din mulţime iese)

GHEBOSUL

(se furişează lîngă trupul mort şi se-ntoarce spre norod cu un rînjet)

A doua oară a venit între voi

Şi nu l-aţi cunoscut.

Ochi ca ai lui nimenea n-a mai avut   390

Şi nu l-aţi cunoscut.

Apropiaţi-vă, priviţi-l!

V-aţi ucis pe Zamolxe cu statuia lui

Nemernici!

Uimire şi cîteva ţipete. Toţi se adună în jurul celui mort. Apoi linişte.)

UNUL

(Lîngă columna din faţă, către vecinul său)

Zamolxe e mort.   395

AL DOILEA

Dar ne-a adus pe Dumnezeu.

ÎNTÎIUL

Orbul e iaraşi între noi.

AL DOILEA

Şi-n noi.

Zalmoxis

He throws himself onto his statue and tumbles it down with his fists.
The people, kneeling all around look on with confusion. They stand.
There is chaos, and shouting: "The Statue," "The god". "Broken",
"Violated altar", "Woe", "Kill him". A couple of shepherds rush over to
Zalmoxis and heave him over. They pelt him viciously with broken
pieces of his statue. The Hunchback emerges from the crowd. He
hurries beside the dead Zalmoxis and then turns harshly to the crowd.

HUNCHBACK

(rushes to the dead body and turns to the people with a cry)

This is the second time he has come among you

and you didn't recognize him.

He has eyes unlike no other   390

and yet, you knew him not.

Come closer, behold him!

You have murdered Zalmoxis with his own statue,

scoundrels!

(Astonishment and some cries. All gather around the dead man. Then
silence)

FIRST PERSON

(standing beside the column in front, addressing his neighbor.)

Zalmoxis is dead.   395

SECOND PERSON

But he brought us God.

FIRST PERSON

The Blind One is among us once more.

SECOND PERSON

And within us.

Doris C. Plantus

The Revolt of Our Non-Latin Nature

The dialectic involving the manner in which Magus conceives the man-nature relationship and that of his conception of Zalmoxis (in fact, the Dacians in the play), and the way this dialectic is expressed in the dialogue between Magus and the Woodcarver recalls with great detail the Appolonian-Dyonisian opposition from the writings of Nietzsche's *The Birth of Tragedy Out of the Spirit of Music.*[1] The opposition established in dialogue between Magus and the Woodcarver thus suggests, as Corin Braga observes, that "...Nietzsche, as well as Blaga, had a good cultural intuition when they used a Dionysiac symbol as the re-emergence of an ancestral nature of a non-Latin substrate."[2]

Lucian Blaga's creative spirit recognizes a reorientation in the moment in which the epoch of its formation concludes: the necessity of his own ethnic spirit's affirmation in rapport with other cultures cannot exclude the implication in the artistic discourse of the human concept of being and the purpose of existence. The objectification of lyricism is realized through cultural masks, evident in the cycles of *The Death of Pan* and *Verses Written on Dried Grape Leaves* from the volume *Footsteps of the Prophet.* In this same context Blaga will take up a new (literary) type, the dramatic poem, in *The Hermit*, included in the volume cited and further advanced in *Zalmoxis.* Among these, *Zalmoxis* remains the one in which attitudes of disconcerting

---

[1] George Gană, Teatrul lui Lucian Blaga, studiu introductiv la Lucian Blaga. Opere. 3. Teatru. (Bucureşti:. Editura Minerva, 1986), XV-XVI.
[2] Corin Braga, *Lucian Blaga. Geneza lumilor imaginare*. (Iaşi: Institutul european, 1998), 185.

strangeness are most easily determined, as a dramatic poem in which each character autonomously structures his own discursive lyric, expressing thus a variety of concepts over the spiritual background of the Dacians.

The charm of each nuance in part reveals the way in which the author chooses to structure theatrically his own dramatic perspective upon the rebellion of our non-Latin foundation. The Shepherd is afraid of the moon's light: "The sun's is light, but the moon is heavy," (*Zamolxe*, I. iii). He re-experiences it as if a burden, inasmuch as the light propagated by the moon is not the true light, the primary one, the original. It is an unnatural reflex of real light, while the state of knowing the singular truth finds itself in a precarious condition, perhaps even erroneous, in that which regards the Dacians, in the example of the Shepherd. He who is struck down during the incident of the moon's light is no longer himself in connection with the real world, in part because the world itself that surrounds him is no longer the authentic one. Thus he is not correctly revealed by a false light. It would be possible to sustain a parallel between the ontological condition of the people of Glaucon's *The Myth of the Cave*, by Plato, and the transformation of the Shepherd's very being under the incident of the moon's light. Both human states find themselves alongside the projection of essential reality. The Shepherd is conscious of his fault, the unnatural transformation of his nocturnal being, and desires to reintegrate into the correct project, except that he does not know the means by which to achieve this. On the other hand, there is a piece of evidence that must not be overlooked: the moon's light, which is "heavy" [and] under whose auspices the Shepherd rediscovers himself disarmed; it constitutes a direct reference to the nocturnal half of the sky of Attica, troubled, represented by none other than the initiating mysteries and the obscure rituals of sacrifice specific to Dionysian frenzies.

The effects of nocturnal lights are among the most fatal for the Shepherd, he, being transformed into a werewolf: "...and in the form of a black beast I rent the sheep of my flock." (I.iii) The Shepherd performs a sacrilege, or more correctly, a pagan ritual, specifically Dionysian: the renting of sheep, *sparagmos*, which presupposes in the subtext a consumption of raw flesh, omophagia, perhaps the culminating point of the Dionysian feeding frenzy, the moment in which the dying faithful of pagan belief of Thracian origin, believe that they can identify with the god Dionysus himself, represented by a goat. The destruction of the limit of human-deification can be manifested through the beatification provocated by ecstasy. The unification of human with animal suggests a return to the chaos of

the world without laws. However, the eschatological dimension, the soteriological one of the same kind that appears only in Orphism, is missing. Dionysism did not convey souls to the afterlife, not even in terms of eternal life or the salvation of souls, but rather it produced an escape on earth to a strange and disconcerting place. The essence of the Dionysian ritual was to better situate oneself through sacralization of human order. Therefore, in the Apollonian-Dionysian opposition advanced by Nietzsche in 1872, the Shepherd is, in Blaga's vision, the dramatic materialization of those two states. The Shepherd, however, was not always the subject of such supernatural experiences:

SORCERER. Since when do you bear this curse?

> SHEPHERD. The seventh harvest of the grapes.
>
> The uneasy throng had gathered in the orchard of the Blind
>
> One to listen to Zalmoxis speak.
>
> I was the first one to strike him with a rock. (I.iii)

The Shepherd numbers his punishment in bacchanalian points of reference, so common to the daily lives of the Dacians, but also to the Dionysian multitudes of the ancient Greek hills. Beyond evidence, the Shepherd reveals himself the apostle of the new faith propagated by Zalmoxis, even if he is not aware of his ritualistic role that consequently interprets him thus. It reminds us in this sense of the Baccante of Euripides, or *Ajax the Telamonian from Salamina* by Sophocles, mortals above judgment through whose reason god exercises his direct will. The transfer of the new faith from this prophet, Zalmoxis, to his first disciple, the Shepherd, will produce itself at the level of thought without voice, without words, through a mere look that will deeply mark the conscience of the first mortal who affects the slightest gesture of abjuration, in denying such an apparent outcast: "I don't know anymore, I trembled and after I ached / because the young man opened his sad eyes, wide— / and did not / ask why. / But on this same night the moon had appeared also. / I tore five sheep to shreds and then I wept in their fleece." (I.iii) In order to convince the community with their own traditions of the authenticity of a new religious faith, Zalmoxis offers a just example of the conversion of his first opponent. The fault of not having recognized the new faith of the Blind One is expiated through grave ontological rumblings. The new god is a vain and vengeful one. His emergence from natural coordinates of humanity tries the character who is both chthonic and Dyonisian with the new religion. Yet all of this can offer a solution to the reintegration into the natural order of humanity, the condition being simple obedience, recognizing your initial error. The Shepherd continues: " I track the young man with the big eyes / and seek in the sand the blood that runs from his body. / When I sip a drop of his spilled blood I come to my senses / and become once more—a man." (I.iii)

The Shepherd is more afraid, however, of the vindictive character of the new god, Zalmoxis, than the authentication of the new faith of the Blind One. The essential need of the Shepherd is precisely to free himself of the incidence of living under the nocturnal auspices: "Protect me from the moon," he implores, appealing to the Sorcerer (the traditional sacerdotal/shaman), proof that the Dacians were not ready to assimilate the new religion of the Blind One. The solution to transform the prophet, Zalmoxis, into one of the gods of the traditional polytheistic religion appears thus rightfully inherent, the only compromise possible for a community unprepared and incapable of being initiated into monotheism. Because the teaching of the Blind One was strange to the Dacians, it proves the fact that the Shepherd seeks an escape by making an appeal to the Sorcerer who, fundamentally is an impostor. By invoking the spirit of the fire, (the first spirit as much in the primordial sense as in the rudimentary), he avails himself of the slyness of rationality in order to denature a dangerous teaching through incomprehensibility and his transforming or reforming condition. "Zalmoxis was not a man" decrees the voice of the Magician, the sacerdot who, intuiting himself through disappearing into neant does not have the power to thwart by means of traditional ritual, but through the illusion of a virtual myth which, once patent, is easily framed in ritual practices, perhaps even adding to them new forms and dimensions, while still guaranteeing survival: Apollonian rituals. Harmony of visible forms was specific to the Apollonian, apparent by calm, serene, unproblematic equilibrium and adeptness to this ontological paradigm seems to be restored in the Shepherd when he partakes of the spilled blood of Zalmoxis, in the form of wine from the skull. Afterwards, he kneels humbly to the new god, following with the offering of sacrificial trout on the altar. Coincidences with aspects of Christianity are omnipresent throughout this dramatic poem.

Reintegration into equilibrated, harmonious data precisely determined as in a cult of the Apollonian type, seems to be realized through the desires and will of the Magician. For the new cult of the Zalmoxis-god isn't the veritable one; it is further clouded by the present parable apparently incidental and negligible in the second act, that is constituted through a facile solution discovered by the children to evade the horrors of reality. Terrified by "the Shepherd who turns into a werewolf at night" the youngest child, Nusitatu, will hear the counsel of the oldest in order to beware the unnatural threat of this strange metamorphosis of a human beast: closing his eyes, it seems to the child already night and that owing to the darkness no one would be able to spot him. In fact, we identify in this existential situation transposed to a ludicrous level, the reactions of the Dacians, who find themselves in incongruence with the essence of the teachings of the Blind One. Fearing this in a similar mode with Nusitatu's fear, they will naively accept an erroneous but convenient stratagem to rid themselves of the dangerous risks to an existential philosophy they would be unable to conceive or assimilate. This would have betrayed the useless vanity of their spiritual condition and would have subjected them to destruction, in metaphysical terms, violating the precise component of beingness that defines them as a human community. The Dacians would close their eyes to the teachings of the Blind One while in a spiritual night they are complacent, so evident because they cannot perceive the truth; they cannot live the religious revelation the way it is very possible to do. This is because not even the Blind One could identify them as virtually faithful. In the voluntarily created nebulousness, it would be easy for them to consider the prophet of a rightful new faith a natural representative of the traditional religious gallery.

In the definitive it is actually well received, being that he is one of theirs, the Getic people, since all of the Dacian deities are of allogenic origin. The Hunchback says, "It is alright like this: from now on you have/ a god who finally understands your language./ The others, after all, speak only Greek," (II.i).

The parallel between the children's game and the community's reaction can be tested also against the level of he who manipulates, here identified as the Magus transposed in "the oldest child", while the Sorcerer is "the middle child." The greatest communities are invested with faith on the part of the youngest, while in times of trouble the youngest needs to believe in the competence of the oldest. He, at his turn, understands this to be his duty to satisfy his pride by manipulating the one situated lower in the hierarchy of the community. An intermediary, the middle child, "clever, holding back his laughter" will exploit the situation inherently created. From the equation all will emerge satisfied and confident, that is, the community is saved in the form of its assembly. What suffers is the principle, the idea that is denatured and its prophet that is spiritually arrested. In 1978, Sextil Puşcariu is the first to observe this aspect at the end of one of the lectures of the play; a lecture realized by the actual author: "...the throngs absent of deep conviction which, in their tendency to divine, forget the idea sowed by the apostle in the moment his statue was raised in the temple."

And still the Dacians were not Greek, but to catalog their faith, whether by the embodiment of the Dionysian, or the regimentation of the Apollonian, implies the denaturing of the true spiritual dimensions that were impossible for them to define in the first place. The most expressive characterization in this sense is offered to us by an intruder, a stranger to the community, the only one who could objectify their being. The Greek Woodcarver would come close to the Dacian being's faith in the Blind One through a difficult rhetorical interrogation:

> WOODCARVER. And maybe this blind god of his
>
> is something else other than this kind of
>
> the Being's and that of the Dacians—
>
> wild, tormented, blind, strange, eternally tried?
>
> Oh, no. I don't feel surrounded by people,
>
> but rather so in the middle of nature
>
> that I wonder how they haven't tufts of moss on the tops of
>
> their heads instead of hair—like the rocks. (II.iii)

Sextil Puşcariu, *Memorii*. (Bucureşti: Editura Minerva, 1978), 533.

With all of this, a conflict between the metaphysical condition of the Dacians and the wisdom of the Blind One is perpetuated throughout the poem, so differences must subsist in both those faiths. A possible explanation is offered by George Gana "...if drawing close to nature is the foundation of the teachings of Zalmoxis and the Dacian's way of being, the understanding or the living of this intimate nearness is different: in the time that his kind live in a natural form (the natural state), the sentiment of the righteous toward her, Zalmoxis brings the awareness of separation and of distance that makes possible the same grasp of nature as a whole, her veneration as a divine absolute (divinization and mythic hypostasis), and her domination, [her] participation in the cosmic through the contemplation of things and through the continuation of the creative process of nature."[4] In fact, the Dacians configured by Lucian Blaga in *Zalmoxis* have a heterogenous character in comparison with the concept of humanity. They are an imperfect construct, their community is undefined, and it is but an embryo of society. The interpretation in conformity with the Dacians, who would have been more than men, is illusory; Dacians appear as something less than men. Their incapacity to frame within a specific divine project need not be viewed as a spiritual failure. Moreover, the Dacians were not yet ontologically completed and thus unprepared for revelation of the new faith of the Blind One. In this context Magus, who orchestrates a work of falsity, need not be quickly condemned. As a spiritual parent, he understands and he worries about his children. In this perspective, the opinions of the Woodcarver

---

[4] George Gană, op. cit., XIV.

and of Magus, apparent contradictions only, admit in subsidiary these states of fact; the ludicrous, infantile character of the Dacians:

> WOODCARVER. O, believe me, with their hearts
>
>   they understand him and even now are close to him.
>
>   But Dacians have the imaginations of children.
>
> SORCERER. If they would live like Zalmoxis wished
>
>   them to, they would consume themselves like fire.
>
>   Children need a gentle dream to calm them—
>
>   and light to stop them from bolting, to hold back
>
>   forces that swarm in their earth
>
>   too fertile in troubled wellsprings. (II.iii)

Magus is fully conscious that the apollinization he professes is the cultic compromise needed to insure "the children" comfort. Magus' action could be inspired by—or put in parallel with—the acceptance of Dionysus in the Greek pantheon, described by Erwin Rohde in 1893 this way:

> ...in order to realize the aspiration of religious universality of which they were unreproachably inspired, his priests [those of Apollo's] had taken under their protection the Dionysian cult. (...) But the cult at whose propagation and,   without doubt, to which the ordering of the oracle at

Delphi had contributed, was a cult of

Dionysus more meek and civilized.[5]

On the other hand, the religious phenomenon called Zalmoxis was a recurrent-obsessive idea of the inter-bellum period, being re-felt like a defining line of the uncertain origins of national specifics. Nichifor Crainic affirms in 1924, in the pages of *Gândirea* in an essay entitled *"Parsifal"* , the contradiction between our autonomous soul and strange forms in the case of the Romanization in Dacia. The Thracian, Dyonisian soul of the "woodsman Zalmoxis", says Magus, the "eternal young woodsman", says Zemora, could not be integrated in a harmonious whole equalized in the forms of the Roman civilization. In Nichifor Crainic's opinion this anti-thesis artificially applied constituted a work of falsification that illustrates the phenomenon of pseudo-metamorphosis: the capture of a primitive soul in foreign or strange forms of a proposed culture. A similar idea had been expressed earlier by the actual author of the dramatic poem in 1921, in the pages of that same journal, *Gândirea,* in the essay "The Revolt of Our Non-Latin Origins". Blaga writes:

We speak of the spirit of our culture;

we want to be only this: Latin—calm,

rational, balanced, lovers of form,

classics—but wanting or not wanting

we are much more; (...) it can be said

that in the Romanian spirit Latinity

---

[5] Erwin Rohde, *Psyche.* (Bucharest: Editura Ştiinţifică şi Enciclopedică, 1989), 244.

dominates quietly and through cultural excellence. We have, however, a rich Slavic-Thracian nature, exuberant and vital, which, regardless how we might resist, it sometimes is freed from the corolla of the unknown, rising powerfully in our consciousness. Latin symmetry and harmony is frequently ripped by a storm that strikes mildly in depths however metaphysical of our Romanian soul. It is a revolt of our Latin essence".[6]

Avant la lettre, Magus' solution to transform Zalmoxis from a prophet of the faith of the Blind One into a god of his cult proper, can be framed in the coordinates of a spiritual falsification, in terms defined by the intellectual thinker. In this context an existential dilemma is born: which of the antinomical ideologies is the authentic, with regard to the absolute? Zalmoxis himself seems caught in this impasse, because he exiles himself in a cave where he waits as if in a maternal womb, like a monad in a virtual [act of] becoming, evolving, living the tortured revelation of incompatibility of the Blind One and the Dacian. He seems to realize that having come at an improper time, into a world not prepared to meet him: "I fear that too soon will I bring a new faith among men." (II.ii)

---

[6] Lucian Blaga, "Revolta fondului nostru nelatin," în „Gândirea", anul I, nr. 10, 1921, 181-182, apud. Lucian Blaga, *Ceasornicul de nisip,* ediţie îngrijită, prefaţă şi bibliografie de Mircea Popa, (Cluj-Napoca: Editura Dacia, 1973), 48.

However, Zalmoxis' emergence into the light is inevitable and inherent. His alter ego, visions of the prophet's actual condition in various states, explains the irreversible: the prophet cannot shirk from assuming his actual irrevocable destiny, he cannot deviate from the pre-established path in conformity with fate. The first avatar, the Old Man, identified with Socrates, admonishes him: "When you are a wellspring, all you can do is run to the sea! / You, Zalmoxis, why do you linger in this cave?" (II.iii)

Not by happenstance does his posture remind him of the subsequent initiator of Christianity, Jesus Christ, the Young Man with "the crown of thorns", certifying his fate: "I bring you news from the other side. Your moment draws near, new man." "The Man on the Stake," evidently the future Giordano Bruno, is the most drastic in formulating without equivocal sentence, the unique possibility of consuming with purpose his passing through life: "Rise up, mankind, toward the sky / or else may the worms gnaw at you in the grave." (II.iii). Though he can intuit his own end—or perhaps precisely because he can from the fragments offered to him, perhaps even by the Blind One, in order to extract him from an impasse—Zalmoxis understands and accepts his fate: *"He storms out of the cave. A great light attends him."*(II.ii) Dramatic transfiguration and the adaptation of the scene in the garden of Ghetsemani did not diminish from the divine project. The tragic condition is not the community's, that perhaps—or not—would thrive outside the predestined information/data of a transcendent principle, the Blind One. The metaphysical condition of the community is no less authentic, even if it is not written in the construct promoted by Zalmoxis. The Dacians can exist in continuation in a specific ontological degree, that of the instinctive, without being conscious that they would be guilty or that they would somehow commit a mistake. The Dacians can be recorded as a conglomerate that does not surpass the limit while their story closes this way. The tragic character still belongs to Zalmoxis, he who is conscious that he has fulfilled a precise, predestined role, a role that the "Thracian public" does not recognize, does not accept. Zalmoxis is thus the only one in danger to fail.

The young woman Zemora, the first to meet Zalmoxis, does not reiterate after a long time waiting for the one in the cave, the performance of the prophet's investment with "the understanding by telling about the beginning of the world." After seven years, at the emergence of the prophet into the light, the meeting between them repeats, but she is no longer the same one. The young woman speaks to the man about a god, without understanding that the very same man gazes into her eyes and that the god cannot exist: "Zalmoxis was too much to behold, / while this is too much man." (III.i) Part of the blame in the virtue of which Zalmoxis can no longer be prophet belongs to the protagonist himself. This can be deduced from a dialogue that refers to the Dacian bard, Madura, a variation on the same fixed theme, the man bestowed with a divine gift to communicate with his kind a fragment broken from the transcendent, when Zemora says, "He lived in his little citadel, all alone, / until he murdered his soul." (III.i) Zalmoxis murdered his soul, his piece of humanity, living in his hermitage in the cave. The auburn horse spied in "the moondust" is the last messenger of what had once been a bard. The stallion does not carry his master in his mad splenetic run toward the castle, an ambiguous and polyphonic symbol of the ivory tower, of the seat of the people, of the localization of a superior instance, of that which cannot be conquered. The lyre/harp he drags in his wake gives the Dacians to understand, apparently, that his divine grace has ended. The harp will never more give birth to delight the redeemed being of Madura, because he has consumed his destiny. The representative question is raised, however, of whose faith—and the metaphysical finalities— is the bard, Madura. Is he an avatar of Orpheus, who bewitches with his charmed lyre the wild things of the woods, establishing thus harmonious forms, serenity, and calm? Or is he a bard from Dionysus' retinue? The music belongs, according to Nietzsche, to spheres of action of this god, inasmuch as the forms of the music stir restlessness in the soul of the receptor, the rhythm of the music sends everything that exists to disharmonic running. Therefore, does the vanishing of Madura signify the establishment of the arbitrary vitalist-organic or, to the contrary, the enthronement of a domination of Being through contemplative co-participation to the cosmos? Does it suggest the failure of the prophet, Zalmoxis, or the failure of the anticipation of the revelation of the Blind One? Why did Madura understand that he has to die to transmit a primordial song, tempera of autonomous metaphysics, to his kind through music, whose melody was already whistled by shepherds for a long time, a song of which Madura would not have to know anything except appropriate words? Specifically, in the "barren horizon" the "ancient secrets" are housed, secrets that cannot be sought through his absent thought. Walking through branches he would be wounded by thorns. The blood of the wound, his pain, would give voice to the harp toward evening not to express necessarily new revelations, but to give the same old secrets the consciousness of eternity. The original mystery of existence cannot be, therefore, overcome: you, as a man, endowed or not, to intuit, however incomplete, imperfect and partial, you are finally forced to let him subjugate you. To recognize yourself bound in face of the mystery means, at most, to know it luciferically, meaning the guarantee of survival of the secret beyond yourself. It is tragedy from hereon in, but all the greatness of the human condition as well, because the ontological destiny of man is to live in the "horizon of mysteries" and to be endowed with "revelation" that is realized through the act of creation, from the prophet. Therefore Madura dies in creation, anticipating the death of the prophet through the revelation of the teachings of the Blind One.

Zalmoxis, however, seems more disoriented than ever with his gaze of his purpose through his passing on the earth. He fulfills, forced by fate, a destiny that surpasses him as an individual. The tracks of his footsteps will earn true [metaphysical] dimensions on the other side of his arduous and ephemeral journey in the world: "And here is my shadow, too—/ I have never understood it. / I cast it from me and still it is greater than I am." (III.ii) The destiny of the prophet, Zalmoxis, would have been to sacrifice himself for his entire people, as a kind of scapegoat over whom he concentrates the sins of the community, sacrificed by people in order to be forgiven and saved by gods. Once they have accomplished the killing of the prophet Zalmoxis, killing even his statue, the Dacians earn the revelation of the myth of the Blind One. Post facto they seem to believe that the Blind One is, from this day forward, among them, theirs, themselves:

FIRST PERSON. Zalmoxis is dead.

SECOND PERSON. But he brought us God.

FIRST PERSON. The Blind One is among us once more.

SECOND PERSON. And within us. (III.iii)

For a similar interpretation Ov. S. Crohmălniceanu seems to agree, that "A type of Dionysian pantheism adapted to theory with a gaze at the Great Anonymous would resume, after Blaga, the religion of the Dacians. (...) In order to arrive at this faith in the mystery that cannot be separated from existence, the Dacians were obliged to stone the prophet to death."[7] In Lucian Blaga's debut play he does not reconfigure the cult of Zalmoxis in his historical markings, but rather creates a space in which the creative imagination of the poet begets his own myth. Mircea Eliade is the one who resumes the synthetic interpretations offered by religious belongings of the Dacian god:

> ... ancient authors as well as modern
> named savants solidarized Zalmoxis on
> the one hand with
> Dionysus and Orpheus, while on the
> other hand with mythical characters or
> mythologized characters whose
> characteristic lines were a technique of

---

[7] Ov. S. Crohmălniceanu, *Lucian Blaga*. (Bucharest: Editura pentru Literatură, 1963), 161.

ecstasy be it of a shamanic type, be it mantic, be it descents into Hell (katabasis)."[8]

And as Florescu notes:

Blaga's Blind One wants to embody two similar dimensions, nature in its fullness of creative capacity, within an attempt to express and artistically reconcile a chronic and perpetual indecision of the reception of the historical reality of the cult of Zalmoxis, seen as a coincidental opposition: "Otherwise, Zalmoxis is a variant of the original name of Zalmoxis with the significance of a god of the earth. It is possible that the metathetical transformation of the name and epiphany take place on the mountain peak, a place specific to the uranic cult, loses its chthonic sense, so much so as

---

[8]) Mircea Eliade, *De la Zalmoxis la Genghis-Han*. (Bucharest:. Editura Ştiinţifică şi Enciclopedică, 1980), 51.

to become confounded with the initial
divination of the Gebeleizis sky.[9]

Between the chthonic and the uranic in Blaga's play, it is possible that Zalmoxis could have lost contact with his kind. Starting from an existential dimension so specific and familiar of his people, namely the chthonic, Zalmoxis will have estranged himself to Dacians through his overstay in a cave, where in his attempt to embrace a new dimension— the uranic—seemed too much to those below, prisoners of their own spiritual limitations, ontological or drastically sanctioned and from within a primary instinct of self-protection. However, the
myth is born spontaneously after the disappearance of the prophet, the intuition and consciousness of the Dacians suggesting a revelation. Sacrificing his messenger, the Blind One has guaranteed his being in the horizon of immortality. The achievement of the dramatic art of the author, found at the beginning of the same road as the poet and as dramaturg, can be considered, without reservation, the gathering of the world in cosmic perspective, the intuition and expression suggestive of the absolute foundation of man, the relationship of the human being in rapport with the nature of the universe.

Lucian Bâgiu

August 2001,

Mühlbach, Transilvania

---

[9] Radu Florescu, *Note la Vasile Pârvan, Getica.* (Bucharest: Ed. Meridiane,1980), 540.

The Two Zalmoxes

"The Getae are the most brave and just of all the Thracians (...) After [the] Indians, the Thracian people are greatest in number; if they had a single leader and were united in mind, they would be, in my opinion, invincible."[1]

"These people are of course too small to be able to ever think about territorial expansion and imperial foundations, but *theirs is a destiny of the other kind of expansion...the most beautiful of all expansions...the expansion towards Heaven.*"[2]

The Problem

"We speak of the spirit of our culture...the marked percent of Slavic and Thracian blood that boils in our being, constitutes the pretext of a problem, which should be put forth with the greatest daring."[3] That is how the young Blaga put it in an article that appeared in the same year as *Zalmoxis*—1921, in *"Trilogia cosmologică."* The special incisive tone of the article (in distinct contrast with the otherwise quiet and melancholy Blaga), addresses the "fierce worshippers before the altar of Latinization," and "[these] partakers of the past, are brought to blows with their dry, or unbridled positivism." His reference to the bacchanal exuberance of a life evolved outside the space of the text,

---

[1] Herodotus, *Histories, IV,* trans. Adelina Piatkowski and Felicia Van-Stef (Bucharest: Editura Ştiinţifică, 1961). N. pag.

[2] Lucian Blaga, *Izvoade*, (Bucharest: Editura Humanitas, 2002), 75.

[3] Lucian Blaga, *Trilogia cosmologică*, (Bucharest: Editura Humanitas, 1997), 511.

makes us question if perhaps the problem which [he] invites us to join, was not much more than a banal conundrum in passing for the author. That is, not the sort of problem to which we fall victim once in a while that makes us partisans to ideas we find strange; instead, the kind of idea that we barely recall after a short time, if at all, when other distractions will have infused weave a whiteness through our cultural receptiveness to the daughters of the Moment. It is true, the same kind of a-perceptive accent would touch young man of 26 years of age often, for as many as the author had at that time. And maybe the tendency to perceive things this way ourselves might draw us in, (shaking off the complications of useless hermeneutics), if we wouldn't come across, in the fragment below from *"Gândirea,"* some of the "places" which, taken in the context of the Blagian ensemble of creation during his youth, explain everything:

> ...in the Romanian spirit Latinity dominates, peaceful in its cultural excellence. We have, however, a rich Slavic/Thracian base, exuberant and vital, which no matter how we deny it, breaks free sometime from the corolla of the unknown, rising powerfully in our consciousness. The Latin symmetry and harmony is frequently to us tangled by a storm that flashes slow

> lightning   in   depths   however
> metaphysical of the Romanian soul.[4]

The metaphysical depths of the Romanian "soul" and "consciousness" represent in Blagian vocabulary, terms of major significance, defining his intellectual style, and the mode in which he chose, (or how he was chosen) to valorize cultural existence.

For us, it has become clear that the problem to which the philosopher refers is a problem of consciousness, one of such implication that any attempt to answer, causes one to become the implicit author of a grave exercise of defining the Self. Lucian Blaga's problem was at that time his, as well as that of the people through whose layers he felt he had emerged.

After the war, the victory of Romanian political independence impelled the consciousness of the bearers of the national message toward the fulfillment of a higher ideal. *Primum vivere, deinde philosphari.* After centuries of imperial servitude, the remaking of the national corpus asked for a spiritual integration as well. Romanians did not want simply to be. They wanted to be they, themselves. They wanted to find the meaning of their existence. And to find this in particular, an entire Pleiades of exceptional intellectuals hurried to bring their contributions. In this, there was an imperative need of definition along a horizon that exceeded the sphere of individuality. They tried to find themselves one with a people to whom they belonged organically. This produced the very moment to which we now

---

[4] Lucian Blaga, *Revista Gândirea* I.10 (1921), 181-182.

refer as having no other historic equivalent. Looking back from where we are today, we understand the glory and the tragedy of this post war generation: glory—because of that which they were given to live, because of the enormous joy of trying, and for successfully opening the wells from the very springs of their people. Tragic—for the pain of seeing their dream crash not in some uncertain future, but rather beneath their very eyes, under the soviet boot, both political and anti-metaphysical; a blessing and a curse. Lucian Blaga was one among them. Neither the blessing nor the curse would spare him.

Casting a glance loosened from prejudgments of the past, Vasile Băncilă, writing in *"Tiparnița literară"* another brother of that generation, condemning the "caddishness" which he sees in culture as nothing more than "intellectual sport," something not serious, thus, deciphers in this atmosphere an "integral attitude that should unify the conduit confronting the eternal problems, with those regarding social problems."[5] The agent of this new generation, it appears, wants an attitude. He does not want merely a contemplator of the demonized present, as much as one capable of establishing a direction. He longs not so much for a savior, as he does a savior of reality, and his seriousness is of cosmic proportions. These youth thirsting for the absolute all visited Socrates' school and Dostoevsky's too. They learned that the single truth worth fighting for and dying for is existential truth, and they realized quickly that one does not reach this truth except through a profound interior transformation. With this, we arrive at Dostoevsky, where Lev Șestov, in *Filosofia tragediei* admits

---

[5] Vasile Băncilă, *Revista Tiparnița Literară* 2, nov. (1926). N. pag.

likewise that the only path that leads to truth is "subterranean."[6] This inter-bellum generation was in truth, a subterranean generation.

The spirit of the Romanian people was still a "sleeping monad" writes Blaga, in "*Trilogia cosmologică*."[7] It would follow that it would awake to life by the shouts of these young people. But they were not yet schooled enough to understand how to guide these interior demons. As Nichifor Crainic said in *Gândirea*, they searched everywhere but could find only "professors," [and] even if they were of exception, they were still "incapable of setting a blaze to scientific mountains with a lightning-drenched aurora of some of the greatest and best developed arguments."   In no case did a spiritual master present himself. Not one guide.   Therefore, no one among the contemporaries could help them. And yet, guidance existed: one came from the past—it was Tradition, but taken in a different fashion than apprehending it merely as a point of orientation that could bear seeds. The other was super-temporal in the figure of the Teacher Christ. All of them lived, as Petre Tuțea has remarked, "between God and people." But to seek tradition, means to seek the essence of the notion that "it could be so." Critics of traditionalism came late only to the historical phenomena of tradition, that which History was able to give. And here they had a right to criticize—Romanians didn't offer a great history, in whose delta, returning, we should refresh forces. Tradition is sought at [its] wellsprings. These wellsprings were those of the Romanian spirit, just as innocent, just as fresh in those times as in the beginning. Revisiting the question sometime later, Blaga would write: "...we need

---

[6] Lev Şestov, *Filosofia tragediei* (Bucharest: Editura Univers, 1997). N. pag.
[7] Lucian Blaga, *Trilogia cosmologică*, (Bucharest: Editura Humanitas, 1997), 511.

not search for our originality in that which we like to name our history. Our originality is somewhere beyond this history—which is not a true history. Our originality—to be gathered through intuition but not formulated—is still on that plain, the other side of essences and not in the phenomenality of our pseudo-history,"[8] (*Trilogia cosmologica*). A possible wellspring of this type was also the legendary Zalmoxis, but another Zalmoxis than the one usually remembered by history; a spiritual Zalmoxis, contemporary with the days of Genesis.

The key to understanding Zalmoxis (and, in fact, all of Blaga's creations during his youth), is precisely the problem to which we refer. Whoever does not admit this perspective fails to understand Blaga, exactly as most of our critics have: the key to understanding Blaga is not demonism, as Alexander Paleologu thought, evidenced in *Spiritul şi litera: Incercări de pseudocritică*.[9] The key is the new spirituality, by which the Poet-Philosopher felt touched. Reticent as Blaga was, however, he did not give us many indications of what he fully meant. His stinginess on this issue has become, in fact, proverbial. But he had a moment where he spoke freely, without having to hide behind his characters or his own silence. In November of 1928, Petru Comarnescu completes an "investigation" whose results he will publish in *Tiparniţa Literară*.[10] The question posed to the great personalities of the times was: "Have you observed in your preoccupations or in those of the entire culture, signs that would support belief in a new spirituality of a deep and general significance?" Peer-review data being rather scarce

---

[8] Lucian Blaga, *Trilogia cosmologică* (Editura Humanitas, 1997), 511.

[9] Alexandru Paleologu, *Spiritul si litera: Incercări de pseudocritică* (Bucharest: Cartea Româneasca), 1970. N. pag.

[10] Petru Comarnescu, *Revista Tiparniţa Literară* 2, nov. (1926). N. pag.

regarding Blaga's particular creations, we will cite here Blaga's entire reply:

> New spirituality exists. So much so that
> I do not feel I exist except through it.
> For my part I have tried to nurture the
> myth in all [my] poems, the
> metaphysics of sleep in the last of
> them, "Zalmoxis' Blind One," "Jesus-
> Earth," "The Anonymous Luke," [and]
> "Manole's Sacrifice." How well I
> achieved this, I do not know, but it is
> certain that all my friends wear a
> halo.[11]

Historic Fact and the Blagian Opusculum

In the epoch of reform brought by Zalmoxis to the Geto-Dacian people, the whole world found itself in an historical fever. In Babylon, under Nebuchadnezzar, a tower was constructed to heights whose people had raised their eyes lit up with luciferian pride for the first time; in China, Lao-Tse was opening a path to Dao; Zarathustra the Persian, receives the message of his mission; Ahura Mazda, the wise lord, is depicted in a personal way, opening the path to "the Good Religion," the very religion that would cause many fits of intellectual epilepsy for the philosopher Superman; Gautama Buddha, founder of

---

[11] Lucian Blaga, *Revista Tiparniţa Literară* 2, nov. (1926). N. pag.

Buddhism, shows us the true path to Illumination; the philosopher and moralist Confucius reminds people that man, a particle out of all Nature, a miniature cosmos, has within himself all the characteristics of Dao: order, justice, goodness and sincerity; in the capitol of Rome, the "She-Wolf" is installed, having become the symbol of the Eternal City. Therefore, during the period in which Zalmoxis projects into the Absolute the destiny of his people, the greater part of the known world is prefiguring subjective and local dates of their existence in order to transform in universal moments of history. Incidental or not, these moments conform so well as if to obey the laws of this spirit. But before we acknowledge the subtle voice of this [spirit], we should consider first the subtle gurgling of historical wellsprings.

Such wellsprings with regard to the existence and work of Zalmoxis are different, and of an honorable antiquity embodied in celebrities of large prestige: Strabo, Herodotus, Plato, Origen or Clement of Alexandria. Regardless of who the historic person of Zalmoxis actually was in reality, however, according to all of these names in the Cultural Pantheon, we should realize that the perception of him, if only summary, was not reduced to a peripheral one. These noted authors attribute to him some of the most fascinating qualities, such as astronomer, geometer, philosopher, legislator, and medic.

The dazzling historian of antiquity, Herodotus, explains that the Geto-Dacians had found themselves in abject poverty, being without learning, while Zalmoxis lived for a time as a slave [of] the most wise man of Hellas, Pythagoras. He adds:

...winning his freedom, he would have earned great wealth and, earning wealth, he returned among his own a wealthy man. As the Dacians were living a life of miserable poverty and being as they were without knowledge, this Zalmoxis [...] had them build a room in which to receive and host important citizens; during such receptions, he would teach that not only he, not only his guest, nor their heirs would ever die, but rather they would move to a place, living forever, they would have a part in every goodness. The entire time he hosted his guests, he also had them construct a room underground. When the subterranean chamber was finished, he made himself unseen to the Thracians, while he stayed hidden for three years. The Thracians, meanwhile, were overcome with grief and mourned after him as they would a dead man. In the fourth year, however, he reappeared once more before the Thracians and such is how Zalmoxis made them believe everything he had taught them. Behold the story they [students] told about what Zalmoxis would have done. As for myself, I do not doubt, nor do I fully believe what they say about him or his underground chamber; otherwise, I figure that this Zalmoxis lived long before Pythagoras. Whether Zalmoxis was but a man, or that he was, in truth, a god in Getic lands, I take my leave of him.[12]

The unequivocal Master in the art of philosophy, Plato, speaks of Zalmoxis in *Charmides,* in more admiring terms:

Zalmoxis (...) our king, who is also a god, says further, "that as you ought not to attempt to cure the eyes without the head, or the head without the body, so neither ought you to attempt to cure the body without the soul; and this," he said, "is the reason why the cure of many diseases is unknown to the physicians of Hellas,

---

[12] Herodotus, *Histories, IV,* trans. Adelina Piatkowski and Felicia Van-Stef (Bucharest: Editura Științifică, 1961). N. pag.

because they are ignorant of the whole, which ought to be studied also; for the part can never be well unless the whole is well." For all good and evil, whether in the body or in human nature, originates, as he declared, in the soul, and overflows from thence, as if from the head into the eyes.[13]

About this same Zalmoxis, the historian Strabo, in *Geografia VII*, confesses with great clarity:

A Get, named Zalmoxis, was a servant of the renowned Pythagoras. He attended the illustrious philosopher in all of peregrinations through mysterious world of Egypt, where he acquired precious and secret information about celestial phenomenon, about the human spirit, about geometry, philosophy and medicine. Returning to his own country—free, initiated and wealthy— Zalmoxis quickly had the respect of the rulers and

---

[13] Plato, *Charmides, Opere I,*(Bucharest: Editura Ştiinţifică şi Enciclopedică), 1975, 156D.

the people. Afterwards, he succeeded to convince the king of the Geto-Dacians himself to share power with him, as a superior man, endowed with the gift of knowing the will of the gods. In the beginning, the king entrusted to him the office of High Priest of the gods, after, he proclaimed Zalmoxis a god himself... [14]

Are these mere analogies at the behest of some *zeitgeist* ruler? Perhaps the different accounts were but a blessed coincidence or, maybe the references to Zalmoxis mean nothing, despite what "the poets say," as Aristotle once wrote. Nevertheless, for Blaga, the creator, the historic fact itself, real or merely presumed, does not represent anything more than cultural material of an artistic transfiguration of proportion. When one has something to say, one proceeds from the fact—the precursor of a work, and what is said, becomes the thing that follows next. Therefore, if we want to know who the true Zalmoxis was, we need not ask Herodotus, or Plato, or Strabo, and not even the great historian of religion, Mircea Eliade. If we want to know, we have to say the opposite of Heidegger, who said: "when you go through the forest, you must go through the word forest." We must say: when we pass through a Blagian idea of

---

[14] Strabo, *Geografia VII*, (Bucharest: Editura Ştiinţifică), 1974. N. pag.

Zalmoxis, we pass through the reality Zalmoxis. Before and after nothing else can be found.

Not much time divides us from the superb neo-Kantian saying— where is the universe? The universe is in geography books. *Mutatis mutandis.* Like good receivers who desire to be part of valuable things, we ourselves ask: So who, Sir,

is Zalmoxis? Zalmoxis…? Zalmoxis is that which Blaga says he is. The rest, [are] but stories. And now, we shall speak of the only Zalmoxis we know.

Zalmoxis—Expressionist Drama

Beginning with *Filosofia stilului* (1924) and ending with *Eonul dogmatic* (1931), Blaga, through permanent transmission makes commentaries and analyses with the smack of prophetism above an expressionist current. If for the majority of contemporaries this represented more of a mode being tried out, however clumsily in certain countries of Western Europe, for Blaga, Expressionism represented a milestone in the definition of a future historic epoch. Expressionism wasn't an invention.

Let us explore a couple of positions.

For Mihai Ralea, in his article *"Scrisori din Germania,"* [15] [he claims] "expressionism doesn't correspond to anything precise," since it is more a "disagreeable state of spirit, of epochs of transition" that meets up with the absence of procedures capable of generating a new one. Being bold, resisting conformity, defying what was prohibited—

---

[15] Mihai Ralea, "Scrisori din Germania," *Revista Viaţa Românească* 9 (1922). N. pag.

such things sought after and cultivated in abundance—are nothing more than the result of seekers without fixed point of orientation.

In his *"Semnal teatral"*[16] Tudor Vianu defines expressionism in comparison with impressionism. In the time it takes to reduce a man to a "simple retina," in the case of the latter, the former restores esteem and spirituality. For the expressionist, sensation becomes an occasion for "faith and idealism." Something entirely different happens with Blaga. He speaks of expressionism from the interior. In *Filosofia stilului,* discussing a painting by Van Gogh Blaga observes that "instead of photographing reality rich as it is with its shadows and penumbrae, this deforms it. The expressionist painter will replace impressions from the exterior with "expression loaded with the soul from the inside. "He would never again want to see the painting in reality, but would search for its actual interior image." In a Copernican upheaval, the expressionist would not leave the subject instructed by nature, but instead establish in the painting an interior model. Just as two realities (material and spiritual) belong to ontologically different kingdoms or classes, so too the expression of spiritual states in material works are not possible except through the deformation of the latter. Spiritual states of the expressionist painter are truly interior dramas. They are not reconciled with the self, not at peace, but rather in turmoil of cosmic dimensions. This boils inside and, passed through the material of the work, would create in the receiver the sentiment of a catastrophe of cosmic dimensions. In *Wheat Field With Cypresses,* Van Gogh does not paint the cypresses and fields from the image retained

---

[16] Tudor Vianu, "Nota despre litografia lui Ed Munch: Camera mortuară," *Revista Semnal teatral* anul III-V (1997-98): 76.

on the retina, but flames that erupt from the earth and pierce the threatening skies in fever, and mountains that rise from the dark depths and fields whose movements translate the true demons of the soul. Current reality was annulled in order to surrender a place of superior order. Everything happens as if the soul were in uprising against nature, selecting a different genesis. A receiver

nurtured year after year at the breast of naturalism, would never be in a position to see in a new creation anything but mystic irrationalism and caricature. But Van Gogh isn't a singular case. His manifestations in painting correspond with similar manifestations in other fields—in poetry where it sings "the great starts of the visionary soul", in new relativity physics, where stylization reaches a high grade of abstraction. In painting, the Dutch master is closely followed by Matisse, Picasso and our own Brancuși, in fact. The philosopher says we assist in a process of stylistic congealing, in giving contour to a *nisus formativus*, a striving centered on the value of the absolute. Science and metaphysics worked, each with its own powers to embody a specific horizon of the absolute. Blaga does not say in certain terms, but rather allows it to be understood that the efficiency of the creative act is at its maximum when it finds its place in a specific stylistic camp, and it does not allow itself to be carried by just any Brownian *élan*. The stylistic camp would be the one that organizes the lines of its human force in a Gaussian direction. Collateral enterprises would have no part except to scatter the force and fail.

Returning to the previous idea, exegetes of the expressionist current (plastic arts and literature), did not see in this anything but a cultural manifestation (among others), and sometimes not even that much—only a project that could or could not be possible. Blaga understands in this something altogether different. Here he is no more a worker of the earth (in the prime sense of "culture"), than he is a reader of stars. That is, a prophet. Blaga prophesies what he would prove in later years: the appearance of a new Eon, a long period of the future in human history. But prophets are never satisfied merely to show themselves as the oracle they are, but that they are themselves the first workers. The myth of Zalmoxis speaks precisely of this. But the fact that all his struggles fall beneath the sign of non-fulfillment, of the astrological house of what "was not to be," is paramount in any interpretation of the dramatic poem. "The creative will takes the place of passive inspiration, says the philosopher in *Filosofia stilului*. It is not only the question of those breezes of a new religiosity that pass through us. A vast thought, headed toward creation of a new world, has aroused...A wind of virility...passes through these years..."[17]

The idea of the creative will of history leaves no room for interpretation. But there is another problem: who are the authors of the new creations? The prophet, however informed by divine grace cannot do anything singlehandedly. In order to understand this, we point again to Zalmoxis—despite the fact that he is supported by truth, he could not find a proper compliment to his soul to support him. On the road he would travel, he would find not one apostle, and for this reason he fell. He was but a spark. A stake would have been something else. In *Metamorfoza celui din Nazaret* , an essay published three years

---

[17] Lucian Blaga, "Filosofia stilului," *Incercări filosofice,* ed. Anton Ilica (Timişoara: Editura Faclă, 1977). N. pag.

ahead of *Zalmoxis* in *Voința*, 1921, Blaga speaks about Jesus in terms of how he presents Zalmoxis: "He died because he came too soon." Yet in order that the cry of the prophet should not perish in the desert, there is a need to fulfill a decisive condition: spiritual collectivism. We read "Medieval art...isn't the work of individuals...it is the work of a united spirit that roams over artists" (...). The wisdom of *Vedelor* is a collective work of some thinkers who remained in large part, anonymous" (Blaga).

And more examples continue. Everywhere something great was conceived, there was a need for spiritual collectivism that rediscovered from its Self the anonymous individual. The unification of sight cannot be realized except by dogmatic formulae, whose elaboration the spiritual elite would have to contribute. He who fails atomized individualism would be dogmatic. If the modern epoch is in a profound crisis, it is because of the cult of individuality that was practiced everywhere—"Be yourself!"— is the divide between the Renaissance man up to our present day. There are signs, says Blaga, that the unfulfilled could have very well reached their end. The individual has to get out from under the ill-fated zodiac of individualism and embrace the absolute. Expressionist art, the new metaphysics of the absolute, knowledge with its style—all of this would contribute to the genesis of a new beginning. For this to happen, two conditions are necessary; the first, is to listen to the prophets among us and, the second, to want it to be so. Therefore, this is the horizon from which Blaga perceives when he thinks about expressionism. The element that characterizes most intimately expressionist art (poetry and drama) would be a metaphysical horizon in the interior whose elements are positioned for construction. Expressionist drama is a "drama of ideas". That is why everything that seems to us at first glance a fact and happening to a particular character, needs to be redefined on a metaphysical horizon. In a collection of studies dedicated to the phenomenal expressionist, *Expressionism in Theatre and Art*,[18] Yvan Goll affirms: "The creator has to know of the existence of other worlds outside of the five senses: the superworld. This would not be in any case a backsliding into the mystic or the romantic...although these forms have a common design—*the metaphysic character.*" (italics mine), while Lucian Blaga, adds in his work, *Zări și etape*: "This theatre sketches in evidence upon a metaphysical base."[19] It is necessary, from this point of view to put a philosophical accent on every rejoinder and scenic description if we do not want our lesson to end in caricature!

The critic's eye must support a delicate process of transcendence. If in a single moment we were to fall back into a naturalist perspective, the idea would be compromised definitively. In true expressionist theatre, everything transcends, sometimes, in order to achieve the effect, even logic. We anticipate the example in *Meșterul Manole,* where the central character that embodies the drama in the maximum sense of the creator is not Manole, and not even Mira, but both as one in the same. That is, both—but not playing two different distinct characters; both as one. In other words, the hero of the play is performed by two characters. How can we see one in two? Logic cannot tell us. Again: an eye trained in the expressionist school would

---

[18] Yvan Goll, "Expresionismul în teatru și în arta," *Revista Semnal Teatral* anul III-IV (1997-98).
[19] Lucian Blaga, "Zări și Etape," *Încercări filosofice,* ed. Anton Ilica (Timișoară: Editura Faclă, 1977). N. pag.

have to "see" that over every play and dramatic action the sky makes a curb. When you no longer see it, it has left the dramatic space. That is why a dramatic piece demands a lot. For this reason, Blaga calls our attention in *Filosofia stilului*, to: "The opinion that an artistic piece can be liked immediately, without a preparatory schooling, and especially without passing through intellectual sites, is the invention of childish aesthetics Wouldn't we remain, in this case, forever in awkward perplexity before the revolutionary creators...?. The taste for revolutionary work is imposed."[20]

To see spiritually is to see metaphysically. To see metaphysically means, for example, to see existential drama there where almost everyone sees arguments in a family, as it happens in *Ivanca*. We might ask everyone who was never able to overtake Bogdan Duică: *Who, sir, is the Father? Or Ivanca? What about Luca? Who are these characters who appear to have fallen from another world?* The answer for us, is bound up in a question—they are from another world—the world of the spirit, the Superworld, the Sky. That is why we began the character of expressionism, indicating a "metaphysical base". The term "metaphysic" restores to the idea esteem: transcendence of the physical nature. Continuing [his] ideas of expressionism in *"Feţele unui veac"*, Blaga adds "The characters no longer exist through themselves as individuals, but only as exponents of impersonal powers...pushed through demonic deeds of unloosed

---

[20] Lucian Blaga, "Filosofia stilului," *Incercări filosofice,* ed. Anton Ilica (Timişoară: Editura Faclă, 1977). N. pag.

energies."[21] What naturalist could ever see in the characters Zemora or Daria the soul of the Romanian people? The scenic manifestation of these can never be described by individual psychological reduction or even collectively. Characters of expressionist drama, of the Blagian kind in the first place, are these kinds of supersensitive powers. Many more times than not, these do not have white lines over which to run, but they are contoured in the atmosphere of confrontation with other powers, reaching a cosmic proportion. They are apocalyptic confrontations.

Here is yet another characteristic of expressionist drama that is rediscovered in Blaga. It is not surprising the fact that these types of powers provoked in the individual, bestowed in them a tragic fate. These kinds of fragments of ancestral powers, a-historic in nature, manifest themselves in individuals like Blaga. In order to resist their demonic games, he asks for a body as strong as mountains in *Poezii*. In vain, fate grants only one like ours:

> Give me a body
>
> You mountains,
>
> Seas...
>
> Because your weak clay
>
> Is too tight...
>
> Great Earth, be my trunk...
>
> But I have only you, my fleeting body.[22]

---

[21] Lucian Blaga, "Fetele Unui Veac," *Incercări filosofice,* ed. Anton Ilica (Timişoară: Editura Faclă, 1977). N. pag.

[22] Lucian Blaga, *Poezii*, (Bucharest: Cartea Romaneasca, 1982). N. pag.

Working with this idea in his article *"O încercare de dramă a viitorului,"*[23] Kurt Pinthus asks, what should a reader see in this type of dramatic progression? In no case, he tells us, "the delimitation of a string of action," as much as the energetic progression of "a tragic soul dilated...in the intensity of expression." Without calling on the characteristic psychology of naturalist drama, expressionist drama tries to present in full view the depths of the soul with passion and ardor. The way these depths refuse the constricting effects of rational expression, the affective is called upon. The metaphysical depths and heights are verily solicited, in order to express recourse to the elements of the original emotional-irrational universe. In this sense, Pinthus stresses: "That something of man that cannot be formulated in a scientific manner has emerged in the light with prophetic clarity.

Because of this, the immateriality will boil out if the soul will contaminate the whole world-interwoven with the spirit, without completely spiritualizing. The heroic effort of drama of complete transfiguration of the Universe, and of history besides, will see itself a failure. Materiality that attends an inevitable way the world cannot be annulled. The shell of spirituality, characters repulsed by the invasion of materiality—calcification of the interior, conventionalism, stingy interests and actual impotence of a life lived in the superlative—will bleed under its own exploits. Zalmoxis dies crushed under the weight of his own statue, Manole, at the foundation of the church raised high by only blood and sleeplessness. In the materiality-spirituality binary

---

[23] Kurt Pinthus, "O încercare de dramă a viitorului," *Semnal teatral*, anul III-IV (1997-98): 12.

we have to see the axis of all the tragedies that specify it in each drama.

Blaga lists the following table regarding expressionist drama in *"Filosofia stilului"*:

1. A metaphysic foundation, designed with elements of myth/magic of different religions:

2. Characters tried by existential struggles of ontological dimensions of spiritual élan with visionary transcendence toward another world;

3. Flight from reality reflected in the technique by which they are constructed as unreal, and of hallucinogenic proportions;

4. Rediscovery of the "I" of the author, among the characters of the drama multiplied in varied masks, and many times in competition.[24]

To all of these contour lines we add one more, perhaps the most important. This defining line has much more value than the line of horizon which encompasses but a small part of this—*attitude*.

This attitude is perceived by expressionists as revolt. Kurt Pinthus, in *Twilight of Mankind*,[25] recognizes that a common attitude of poets and expressionist dramaturges fights against an epoch on the verge of ending, concomitant with the healing of a better humanity. Their weapons of combat were "heart, soul and voice". Everyone thought they were the first to announce the coming of another world, a world

---

[24] Lucian Blaga, "Filosofia stilului," *Incercări filosofice,* ed. Anton Ilica (Timişoară: Editura Faclă, 1977). N. pag.

[25] Kurt Pinthus, "O încercare de dramă a viitorului," *Semnal Teatral,* anul III-IV (1997-98): 12.

in which old idols would disappear completely; in other words, a complete renewal. But how might we arrive at this point?

Expressionist writers, certainly Lucian Blaga, repressed the rash of the past with "heart, soul and voice". The past did not willingly yield. There was a need for battle, a need for a revolt, but the revolt of the poets wasn't a political revolt. It was a metaphysical one. The thought and sentiment of this revolt carried on in dramatic works of Blaga, in terms of maximal metaphysic sublimation—a revolt against ontological lies. The terrain upon which this fight was fought cannot be identified on any geographical map of the world. It was a subterranean fear of conscience in whose geometry we find ourselves infrequently enough. From a physical confrontation one can find oneself bleeding, mangled and spread in all corners of the word, but not ontologically threatened. Spirit and soul are touched by no bullets of any army. Meeting the hideous body of Medusa in each of us thus, one cannot emerge but transfigured, overcome metaphysically, even if a single weapon is not discharged.

All of these lines of expressionist drama are rediscovered fully restored, and in Lucian Blaga's first play—*Zalmoxis*.

The Religiosity of Blaga

Whatever autonomy or absence of autonomy a work would have with regard to its creator, who gave it the name among the real, he will never succeed in these two moments—these being the man and his work—a total expression of the whole or the half. Whether it is to make of the work an open book of the creator's biography, or to make of it this moment a perfect transcendence of his self, immediately, these two reductionist attitudes seem to us lacking under the aspect of consequences it would generate. We sooner have to understand the two terms being two moments of reciprocal understanding and, this, within a dialectic game defined in terms of closest and furthest. This is because, in truth, not even man precedes his work, likewise, the other way around. Using a Hegelian algorithm, yet perfectly consonant with the actual hermeneutics of culture, biography and work are born one from the other, each one being the father of the other, and the daughter of the same. And just as the daughter has need of a father in order to exist, so does a father have need of a daughter in order to thrive. What remains is neither man nor work, but a totality at which both have arrived, a totality in which the two are both present and absent.

We have made this excursion, apparently outside the main thesis, precisely to return to the Blagian biographical moment and also to project him into his work, and inverse. Blaga followed his characters in parallel by degrees of knowing them individually.

In *Hronicul şi cântecul vârstelor*, Blaga gives us a veritable spiritual biography of himself. The grafting of this spiritual biography alongside other indicators is one of the keys to understanding him.

He would come to know this state of grace in his native village during the first years of his childhood. Such wondrous phenomena as took place there determined that he would affirm that, he who did not live this childhood in the village would never know it. Everything that signifies both concrete and paradisiacal knowledge, but especially myth and occult, was revealed there. He says as much in his poetry, but especially in *Hronicul şi cântecul vârstelor*:

> Full is the village of aroma of gods like a nest of wild smells" (*"Satul minunilor"*). "Everywhere, from the top of the view, was for me a border, the border of the world...on the other side nothing but...tales...Our thought teaches itself the imperatives from birds to flowers...the hunger of folk tales...only my mother...satisfied...The fairy tale moves from the beginning through a real world, to take it back, on imperceptible steps, toward another realm...I lived palpitating, with my breath arrested here by wonder, there by fear, in the middle of this world...The tale disturbed me for its sweet bitterness with which it spoke about the dawns of joy, but also for the dizzying feeling, which it gave me as I mounted the saddle of the times that rule the world with all her realms as. The village was for me a zone of wondrous interferences: here reality, with its palpable foundations, met with

Doris C. Plantus

stories and biblical mythology that had
in them their own certainties. Angels
and the Tartar of the devils, with their
black children, were for me beings that
themselves populated the world of the
village.[26]

This period was traversed from one end to the other by a specific
religious "inclination", as the author confides, touching threatening
proportions during his early schooldays.

Until the age of 10-11, my life would
be more and more decided by a
religious sentiment, fueled by the most
uncontrollable excrescence. And this,
progressively so. I do not exaggerate
saying that year after year I strove
daily and many times, at least twice, in
prayer, worshipping by any apparent
ritual. I made time and occasion, that
is, for prayer, between the ringing of
the church clock, particularly towards
morning, I repeated in the dark, and
only for an interior ear ten times,

---

[26] Lucian Blaga, *Hronicul şi cântecul vârstelor,* (Bucharest: Editura Eminescu, 1973). N.
pag.

225

twelve times, 15 times, the one and
the same prayer.[27]

After the age of 11 the child was immediately tried by demonic pride: "From wherever until then I fretted because of the abundant interior life of a religious nature...now I alone denounce this mythology." His only perspective was naturalism. The child began to have mature preoccupations with knowledge. He felt an affinity for the materialist, Vasile Conta. Darwinist studies came to him at a moment when his need for the absolute of truth was urgent, as if guided by an invisible hand of fate. Influenced thus by the idea of the material rediscovered in Conta and reinforced by the Annals of the Romanian Academy, Darwinist philosophy and the work that ravaged the intellectuals of Central Europe at that time, *Enigmele lumii* by Haeckel, the young Blaga arrived at the high gate of demonic pride. He actually felt carried aloft by a universal Logos that fed his mind all it craved.

But this period would not last to the end either. Becoming acquainted with different metaphysicians of the world, from Plato to the contemporary Bergson, the sentiment of relativity was planted in his mind. He acknowledged, "Metaphysics became for me more and more a vice without cure, a demonic passion."

Renouncing the Kantian pattern, Blaga began to judge philosophy following the immanent critics—that is, with particular regard to the quality of free creation of the spirit. From here,

---

[27] Lucian Blaga, *Hronicul și cântecul vârstelor*, (Bucharest: Editura Eminescu, 1973). N. pag.

everything entered into the universal equation of creation— contradictory lifestyles, aspirations, projects that would change the world, repeated failures undertaken over and over again. The works he produced during that time, one after the other, whether drama or poetry, seemed a response to this interior crisis.

The demonic attempt did not reveal itself only in drama, but in poetry also. Yet Blaga, for as hard as he tried to break the sky with his fists, remained frustrated and vexed by his search for the absolute. Nevertheless, though fraught with discouragement, he always took up the quest anew.

It is in this phase that we find him working on Zalmoxis, the demolisher of idols and the inventor of the world. In this period he wrote the first seven dramatic works, each one opening an existential circle.

Blaga did not find peace until he assassinated the last prophet. In that moment he understood that non-fulfillment did not mean personal deficiency, but rather a characteristic ontology, thus appeared the myth of the great anonymous one. Beginning with *At the Scales of the Waters*, (1933) through *Demonic Knowledge*, (1933) and *Avram Iancu,* (1934), Lucian Blaga abandons his horizon of demonic pride in favor of integration into mystery.

In the years 1920-1921, well before the moment before Blaga reached his apogee of integration into mystery, he found himself in the full euphoria of pride. The drama *Zalmoxis*, conceived precisely at this time, is punctuated through and through with the fervor of this new religiosity that thrived in Blaga for a second time, after 15 years of negation. This new religiosity, however, had new forms, substantially different from those of a child between the ages of 11-17 years. The first version was a naturalist one. The second was a cultural one. In fact, it was an understanding of culture in absolute terms of consciousness. In articles written at the same time, in the journals *Voința* and *Patria,* he affirms: "All of the epochs of culture...have an idea that borrows the unitarian character of an organism...If we perceive our times...we discover a complete anarchy in that which perceives the cultural ideal. *We are missing the impulse of a single idea that covers all our soulful orientations ...*"[28] In another article he writes, "We are not merely poor beings, but in us manifests a fatality. We call it "a fatality", but it can also be called a "divine order", if our times would be so bewitched with the word of God."[29] Perhaps the most appropriate words come from the article *"Metamorfoza celui din Nazaret"*[30] where he writes, "The years of the past are more mystical, more longing of faith and more noble by the impression of the idea of a fatality that rules the world."

Zalmoxis speaks to us precisely of this fatality. The religiosity of the drama is therefore neither decorative, nor pre-textual. It is the fabric into which the myth will be woven.

The Two Zalmoxis'

We have established that Lucian Blaga wrote his dramatic poem in the style of expressionist drama, with the emphasis on presenting a

---

[28] Lucian Blaga, *Voința*, 87 (1920). N. pag.
[29] Lucian Blaga, *Patria,* V, 33 (1923). N. pag.
[30] Lucian Blaga, "Metamorfoza celui din Nazaret," *Voința*, 56 (1921). N. pag.

new idea. This "new idea" springs from a natural world, and a social world with precise laws and receivers who are obligated to apprehend the subject in the most direct light. But this situation gives way to a paradox: one wants to express a new idea, however,

there is but a single language available predicated upon a collective and ancient body. And? Should one be able to express anything at all within the limitations of such a language? The answer is no. No, because language is not a product of occasional happenings, but rather a result of the very state of things, and in addition to this, there are as many languages as there are individual cultures of people. Therefore, in order to say something new, one must draw from other languages or, at least, give the older languages a new function. The expressionist understood this and adapted accordingly. The expressionist did not create a new language, but overturned the language at his disposition; he deformed it in such a way as to achieve the clarity heretofore unavailable. As some might say, it is necessary at times to adopt a crooked view in order to judge correctly. The purposeful alteration of Van Gogh's painting as a stark contrast to a photographic image of the same subject is imperative to reveal un-natural essences that cannot

be captured by mechanical duplication. Like Van Gogh's paintings, therefore, the drama Zalmoxis risks delivering its message to the eye that perceives it as a naturalist project. Since Blaga was aware of this, having seen himself through these eyes for many years, he gave us a suggestion within the very interior of the play. That is, he introduced in the architecture of the play a deformed character who, though compromised, remains the only character who actually "sees" correctly. We are referring to Ghebos. To see in expressionist terms, one has to see through the eyes of the deformed, the eyes of Ghebos, the Hunchback. Despite the fact that he has very few lines, his speak the truth. He is the only one who chastises the neophytes who chant in adoration the installation of the god, Zalmoxis, when earlier they themselves had cast the first stones that drove him out from among them. He alone follows the brooding prophet into the fortress who, otherwise, finds not one friend in his path. Finally, he alone opens their eyes to the identity of Zalmoxis after he is struck with "holy" stones: This is the second time he has come among you / and you didn't recognize him. / He has eyes unlike no other, / and yet, you knew him not. / Come closer. Behold him! / You have murdered Zalmoxis with his own statue, / scoundrels! (III.iii)

Here, if we are convinced that we will not err if we follow Ghebos, we may cast a quick expressionist eye over the first Blagian drama that tries to homogenize the deformation to which he was subjected.

In the first place, as a consequence of the fact that *Zalmoxis* is a veritable work of expressionism, a drama of ideas, the characters will no longer represent entities and bio-psycho-socio-cultural identities, that move in determinant times and spaces, but rather ideas freed of these very coordinates. The transcendence of space and time become possible because of the very fact that the ideas no longer depend upon them; they are liberated of any material determinism. Precisely behind the most representative characters of the drama ideas are hidden. In this sense, we decipher from the characters the soul of the Romanian people (Zemora), the expressionist receiver (Ghebos), the Hellenist philosophy of Alexandria, the creator of dogma (The Greek Woodcarver), the official church (Magus), the free spirit (the first

Zalmoxis, the Old Man, the Young Man, the Man on the Stake), and the apostle (The Shepherd).

In the second place, the metaphysical foundation of the drama is guaranteed from the onset of the play. The opening scene itself, with the monologue by Zalmoxis, would be, according to the majority of Blagian interpreters the most poetic insertions in the metaphysical pantheon. Even if we would interpret the scene in a totally different spirit, as we will recall, the philosophical framework of the description would remain untouched. And not even as regards the opening of the play, but from the first word until the last. Because this metaphysical frame is designed with mythical-magical elements borrowed from different religions, as apparent in the text, of the Geto-Dacians and Hellenist cultures, for example, the chorus of Bacchante, the Sorcerer's charms, the procession of the installation of the god's statue in the sanctuary, the weeping of Dacian women on the occasion of a new birth, the tossing of young men upon spear-points, etc., this truth is sufficiently expressed in the structure of the drama.

In the third place, the characters of the play no longer live a repetitive dramatic banality, neither individually nor collectively, and neither psychologically nor socially. They no longer expound purely and simply a subjectivity in public or private space, the way they do in representations of boulevard theatre, so well known in the epoch of dramatic writings (and in rapport with Blagian characters seemed to have just arrived from a hospital for nervous diseases), but are tried with existential sufferings of ontological dimension, of spiritual *élan* with visionary transcendence toward other worlds. We have but to consider the second scene of the second act, at the meeting between

Zalmoxis and the three visionaries—The Old Man, Socrates, The Young Man, Jesus, and the Man on the Stake, Giordano Bruno—on the other side of time and space, and our affirmation would be completely covered. We no longer recall the apotheosized ending of the mystery pagan, he, who in fact, confers sense to the whole drama, and in whom the features of the admirers change instantly like an imaginary mountain of Tabor, before the god inanimate, gather around Zalmoxis the man, and looking into his eyes and heart, as they are and not as others would want, succeed in catching a glimpse of him passing closely by God, Himself.

In the fourth place, the flight from reality (called by us deformation of reality), reverberates throughout over the technique with which the characters are constructed. As we said earlier, we have to do with characters that seem unreal, characters of a hallucinatory proportion. And of all the characters, from a distance, Zalmoxis is the most unreal and super-proportioned. Taking God, the Great Blind One by the hand, he assumes a stature of cosmic justice. By comparison, Atlas was still sucking milk from the breast of Clymene, while Sisyphus was playing at climbing and descending hills. Capable of making mutiny of the mountains against its people with the understanding of a child, "he takes upon his shoulders" the fate of divinity, this Zalmoxis is no longer a part of the human category, not able to be figured into a statistic of any kind of census affected among people. At the same time, Zalmoxis is just as warm as any among us. But his body bleeds abundantly beneath the fists with which we protect the minor being, that is, non-being, of invasion into our lives of the Unknown One.

In another sense, Lucian Blaga is not just the author of a "pagan mystery," keeping himself elegantly at a distance from the fate of any of his characters. If he had written purely to amuse or distract us or himself, with certainty, it would still had been his position in rapport with what was going on in the interior of his writings. And his name, as well as his personal implication would have stopped with the inscription on the cover. But it isn't this way at all. Whoever would think so, would be speaking about an entirely different person, one who happened to have the same name. Blaga is no stranger to the lives of his characters. He uses the drama to reveal an interior drama. He doesn't write because he has an idea, he writes to discover an idea. He doesn't write because he is enlightened, rather he writes to become enlightened. Therefore, writing isn't the scope, but rather the author's medium through which he might discover the solution to a problem. Just as a medical treatment tries to cure an illness: "Brother, a disease cured seems to you any kind of book...With this page I close the door and remove the key."[31] And this is why we began this present essay with the subheading of "Problem." Blaga is full of problems. Great and trying problems. Yet the works he has written always follow.

Zalmoxis can be interpreted in many different ways. Some have not managed to see any more than a historical drama, an attempt at a reconstruction in a spiritual manner of a past forgotten, against which the documents appears extremely stingy. Others have read it as a Romanian dramatic response to the myth of Nietzsche's *Zarathustra*, or a bacchanal dance to the classical music theme of opposition between

---

[31] Lucian Blaga, "Încheiere," *Poezii,* (Bucharest: Cartea Românească, 1982). N. pag.

Apollonian and Dionysian forces. And still others, among the author's contemporaries, perceive an unconvincing literary attempt. The philosopher Constantin Radulescu-Motru, the author of the monumental work *Energetic Personalism,*[32] considers the drama as being poor only in lyricism and dramatic breadth, but actually just as wanting in philosophical substance, retaining rapport only with Nietzsche. Mihail Iorgulescu[33] rediscovers in the unfolding of the drama simply a conflict between the human and the divine, while Ion Sân-Georgiu,[34] the first critic who brings to the discussion the expressionist theme in art, does not reveal himself the least bit impressed by the work, declaring it a conscious imitation of German expressionism and even literary theft. The eminent historian, Nicolae Iorga,[35] in unison with all these repulsive positions with regard to *Zalmoxis*, rejects the piece with vehemence difficult to imagine for someone who, not long before, elegized the first volume of Blaga's poems, *Poemele luminii*. Of the entire play, the professor recalls nothing but a small hilum: *"Zamolxe' God, the Blind One, is water that washes over our foot, while the author, a perverted talent."* Ovidiu Densuşianu,[36] also considers the work an epigonic product of new German literature, a cold tale in which dramatism is absent, the scenes without organic communication between them, being nothing more than artificial pastings of moments written in isolation. Moreover, the work does not succeed in giving an authentic image of the Romanian spirit, showing itself estranged to

---

[32] Constantin Radulescu-Motru, *Teatrul* (Bucharest: Editura Minerva, 1984). N. pag.

[33] Mihail Iorgulescu, *Teatrul* (Bucharest: Editura Minerva, 1984). N. pag.

[34] Ion Sân-Georgiu, *Teatrul* (Bucharest: Editura Minerva, 1984). N. pag.

[35] Nicolae Iorga, *Teatrul* (Bucharest: Editura Minerva, 1984). N. pag.

[36] Ovidiu Denuşianu, *Teatrul* (Bucharest: Editura Minerva, 1984). N. pag.

anything that could have relevance with our lives. Scarlat Struțeanu,[37] with whom we will close this gallery of sacred monstrosities, reads in Blaga's pagan mystery a poetic idea that fails to be artistically incorporated with characters unable to be defined, and who have but an anecdotal role in the development of the play. In short, a linguistic product that, in spite of the fact that it is harmonious and archaic, does not finally become a poem. The list of these distaining attitudes towards the dramatic poem, from the quarters of personalities of that time period, leaves room for some bitter conclusions—all of them were missing something. Perhaps not intelligence, since we are dealing with people highly instructed, and even genial in their own areas (for example, Iorga). Perhaps not even attention to the reading, based on the fact that the poet-philosopher from Lancrăm succeeded in attracting them through his previous volumes. Certainly, they were missing the very thing that has the gift of transporting one directly into the hot center of this creation—Love. Just as Tudor Vianu has repeated many times, "...criticism of the Blagian works is an act of love." Thus if there is no love, neither can understanding exist.

Over time, things evolved, love began to grow, and at once with it, favorable criticism. Today, as much in Romanian critical literary circles as well as in other countries, we receive as a reaction to this creative work, only words of praise. An entire literature has commenced in order to restore to the author and his works the esteem they deserve. That is why today there is a firm point of view that conforms Blagian

---

[37] Struteanu, Scarlat. "Aparatul Critic," *Teatrul* (Bucharest: Editura Minerva, 1984). N. pag.

drama in general, and *Zalmoxis* in particular, that numbers among the highest examples of Romanian literary genius.

One additional explanation is offered, one that can open a new direction to the literary critics who have made it thus far. We believe one way or another, that Herodotus has not been overtaken even today. Because what he relayed about Zalmoxis, sent from Halikarnassos, has become so ingrained in our cultural mentality that we are incapable of seeing beyond it; because the letter of the work has mastered the spirit, nevermore allowing freedom to move within the economy of interpretation. The proposition of the new interpretations to which we aspire, proceeds from the intuition that in the discursive structure of the drama, they are revealed, and speak both the parts of two Zalmoxes. In fact, the two apparitions in

the fortress of the prophet are so different from one another that we are directed to conclude that they are not part of the same character. The first appearance in scenic succession is, in fact, the first Zalmoxis, after a suggestion by Blaga himself, the Zalmoxis of yesterday, while the second appearance, comes after an interval of seven years, the Future Zalmoxis. Herodotus limits the interval between these two Zalmoxes by only three years:

> The entire time he hosted guests and
> gave counsel, he had tasked them with
> building an underground chamber.
> When the chamber was completed, he
> made himself unseen in the midst of
> the Thracians and remained hidden for

> three years. The Thracians were
> overcome with regret and grieved after
> him like a dead man. In the fourth year
> he reappeared among them and in this
> manner Zalmoxis made them   believe
> in everything he said...[38]

No one asked themselves why these three years for Blaga became seven. If he prefigured so many elements of historic record from antiquity, why then did he not include this? One thing we know for sure about Blaga; these so-called deviations from history, whether historic or folkloric, are never without a purpose. In fact, these alterations are suggestions the author filters through us within the play in order to help us orientate our reading according to other hermeneutic zodiacs. For us, the cipher "7" equivalent to the seven days of Genesis lets us know that the interval of his vanishing is not a temporal one, but a cultural one. It is an eon that divides one from another—the historical configuration of men who were, from those who will be. The Zalmoxis of yesterday is a prophet of an eon that has exhausted its potential to thrive, a cultural era that has become putrefied. The Zalmoxis of tomorrow is a prophet of a new eon, on the road to its birth. It is like when after a cycle of seasons frozen in the glaciers of winter, the spring, with its explosive vegetation comes to announce the birth of another world. And inasmuch as these eras have

---

[38] Herodotus, *Histories, IV,* trans. Adelina Piatkowski and Felicia Van-Stef (Bucharest: Editura Ştiinţifică, 1961). N. pag.

nothing in common with each other, neither are their prophets capable of taking each other's place.

Conflicted, the first Zalmoxis, as tempestuous as he is an artesian fountain, descends the sacred mountain of Kogainon in order to bring the Dacians a dream that has never been dreamed before. The God alongside whom he walks, is an unknown God: "A new and robust religion tried I / to bring you / from the heart of the Unknown One, (I.i.) wandering through the world's bramble. He is a God who, falling, scatters constellations of light all around him, but whose fall and ascension could become that of the Dacian. Thus measure for measure, throwing the idols who have bewitched him out of his heart, he will choose to take God by the hand and follow his destiny to its end. The first Zalmoxis, carrying that transcendence which released him of any contact with the materiality of the world, confiscated only by the cosmic dream with the force of fatality, a force against which he could not resist, is also one of the rebels in the revolt ("Wasn't I gentle enough? ...There was a time when I howled. I wanted to rebel against even the mountains..."). (I.i) Toward this kind of existence the Zalmoxis of yesterday urged his blood brothers to take steps, abandoned by fear that would have stopped them from throwing themselves into its arms as if onto a large spear. Magus knows this. He understands. But he also knows the fact that the Dacian is not prepared to support this kind of contact with consuming divinity. In the secret conversation he has with the Greek Woodcarver, his cultural function is to domesticate the flames of passion just as Greek Alexandrine philosophy did with its wild teachings of the first Christians. Magus, therefore, clearly denounces Zalmoxian idealism: "If they would live like Zalmoxis wished them to, /

they would consume themselves like fire. / Children need a gentle dream to calm them—/ and light to stop them from bolting, / to hold back forces that swarm in their earth / too fertile in troubled wellsprings." (II.iii)

The prophet's meeting with the very people who would not accept him the first time would result in Magus' vision, with a proportionate disaster: "Either he will perish or the people will." (idem) On this occasion Magus was correct. In truth, the first Zalmoxis died, reduced to nothing not by the stones the frightened Dacians hurled out of the new existential perspective he proposed, but by the his very own cosmic spark that manifested in him for which no man is ever prepared to achieve. He died because he arrived too soon. He was a projectile of a man thrown past himself, an emergence from self that could only end in tragedy. The Zalmoxis of yesterday, of pure love and light purified by any last trace of materiality, was overthrown by the other world of fear and materiality. That is how the others were overthrown---Socrates had to drink the bitter drink of the peace and idol worshippers ; Jesus, of the masses infuriated by His teachings which burned within them, yet who could not understand, while Bruno, was forced to drink the *magister dixit*, whose official diplomas are sought after with such determination by lovers of social status. It is interesting how history conserves itself on the horizon of man. Socrates dies in Plato, that is, in the Universal, Jesus in the Alexandrine philosophy of letters, Bruno in the science of Galileo-Newtonian of brute fact. Magus knows well how important the role of the masses is in the same kind of accommodating equation: "The blameless flock has so distorted him that today even he wouldn't recognize himself." (II.ii) The common name of the art of

239

murder is perversion. History cannot assimilate anything but that which perverts, that which falsifies. It is exactly this that Magus does. The text *Zalmoxis*, if it were written in the form of a treaty, capable of preserving actuality, could just as easily be named *The History of a Perversion*. This is because we find in the entire drama all the elements by which cunning needs to win. From the Magus who reveals the appropriate idol, continuing through to the Sorcerer who finds the Apostle propagandist—the Shepherd—who is ecstatic over his own divinity, with a system of perception that will be offered to the masses (the statue made by the Woodcarver), concluding in the assembly worshipping frenetically at the altar of Normalcy: the Chorus of the Bacchante.

The central engine that realizes the lie is Magus. The others are a mere extension of him. They are instruments. In terms of Blaga's mode of character development, Magus is the one best defined: "The high priest has such a piercing look / he can see through to your thoughts." (I.ii) "In the darkness he has the eyes of a wolf / glowing embers in the wind," (idem) he seems not to sleep ever. Cold, "Bloodthirsty as the holy lessons of today and all times," (idem) he works his plan with great patience and clam, building the body of the god, by alternative course of "sparkling scales" and "eye of snake." From a Christian perspective, Magus has all the attributes of one who adores the fallen divinity, the Anti-Christ. But here the fallen divinity represents nothing more than the pressing of service to brute materiality. Magus doesn't believe in God. The gods he does invoke are but stone idols before those who sacrifice the will of man. Magus' temples are "widowed of faith" just as his heart is. Magus' negativity, nevertheless, has a soteriological function. Paraphrasing what Blaga suggests, we too can say that the role of Magus is to tempt us with his statue, inasmuch as the only road to the future Zalmoxis passes closer to his statue than any other road. In Hegelian language, Zalmoxis of yesterday is a formula of his interior self. The first Zalmoxis isn't [Zalmoxis]; he merely wants to be. He has not of himself being, but the promise of being. This is why Magus defeats him so easily. Magus is the moment of the first negation. The negation of the sky is the earth, rocks. If the first Zalmoxis didn't exist, then Magus' existence could not be justified. Magus defines himself through a negative rapport with the other. If Zalmoxis is pure interiority, Magus is pure exteriority. In the second place, this negativity is not eternal. It asks, at its turn to be overtaken, negated. This is how the negation of negation seems in the person of the second Zalmoxis. Negating Magus, he returns to the first Zalmoxis. But not as he was, that is, in the form of his interior self, but enriched by the moment of history's exteriority. Now he becomes real. The actual smashing of his statue (that of the first negative by the second), brings back a state of normalcy in the lives of the Dacians, (and of ours).

It is fitting to say a few words about the Zalmoxis of tomorrow, of the future, with some summaries justified in the text. The drama opens with his monologue, mistakenly interpreted by critics as a proof of some pantheism to which Blaga would subscribe. But not even here is there evidence of anything of the kind. This type of simplification doesn't even enter into Blaga's preoccupations. Blaga is making literature, not ideology, the way superficial critics would wish. But then what can be induced in their error? The fact, we think, of a unilateral interpretation of the mode in which he describes his relationship with the world, the *incipit* of the drama, that of the second Zalmoxis. He says: "My Spirit—mine and the earth's is just as much as this... (I.i); I've forgotten the difference between me and things that surround me." (idem). Nowhere does it say anything about the Spinozian *Deus sive Natura*. If he would have identified God with Nature, he would never have written on the first page of the drama "Nothing is strange to me, and only the sea am missing." (I.i.) If [God] were identical to Nature, then [Zalmoxis] would not be missing anything. There is another meaning to this so-called Zalmoxian-Blagian pantheism. The first Zalmoxis moved over the concrete world the same as the Spirit of Genesis in the cool of the evening, transcendent and not imminent. This is pure transcendence. One-hundred percent Uranian. Magul is the perfect identification of Nature, but with a divine breath. The future Zalmoxis has from each a little something. He recuperates the exteriority, gathering it to himself. He is a wise Zalmoxis: "and over my days without end has settled a bedrock of wisdom..." (I.i.) "A lake calmed by days without wind, am I," (I.i), "...but today my venom has subsided," (idem). When you are a child you see everything from your point of view, egocentric. When you mature, you have a centrifugal tendency to separate from yourself and perceive everything from the outside, the exterior. When you get to old age, you return to yourself again but only after a long detour made through exteriority of which you would feel at first, strange. That is why it is said that a wise old age accepts everything. That is also the last Zalmoxis. Wizened. But it should not be understood that this Zalmoxis has also arrived. This is a future to be delivered. Blaga gave the drama a conclusion that has not yet taken place, but rather remains to be...it is that which we wish it to be. We have need yet of a savior. In the drama *Zalmoxis*, he only sketched a summary portrait. As stated previously, the new Eon is only on the path to birth. At its arrival, the prophets, people of exception have an important role. But they cannot do it all themselves. We must unify and ask with a collective voice for the Future. Otherwise the expansion to the sky will remain but a lonely dream that will continue to haunt our historic nights of history. Otherwise, we will continue to live in a world of gods who lack nothing but...gods.

Valeriu Sofronie

Professor of Philosophy

Al. Vlăhuță, Râmnicu Sărat, Romania

2010

An Introduction to Blaga's Philosophy for Readers of *Zalmoxis*

In his excellent preface to the current volume, Keith Hitchins mentions, but does not describe in detail, the philosophical system created by Blaga as a compliment to and source of his drama and poetry. In her forward, Doris Plantus, the translator of *Zalmoxis*, likewise alludes to the philosophical undercurrents present in Lucian Blaga's literary works in general and in *Zalmoxis* in particular. I would like to briefly outline this philosophical system for the readers of *Zalmoxis*.[1] I desire to do so – and the translator has invited me to do so – because, while Blaga's poetry is not slave to his philosophy, it is influenced by his philosophy, and understanding the latter will facilitate understanding and appreciating the philosophical aspects of the former.[2]

Blaga's Intellectual Formation

Mircea Eliade, the famous anthropologist and philosopher of religion, described Blaga in his entry on Romanian philosophy in the *Encyclopedia of Philosophy*, as "The most gifted and critical original

---

[1] I have described Blaga's philosophical system in much greater detail, though not exhaustively, in *The Metaphysics of Religion: Lucian Blaga and Contemporary Philosophy* (Madison, NJ: Farleigh Dickenson University Press, 2006).

[2] While it is true, as Hitchins points out, that there is an obvious connection between Blaga's literary works and his philosophy, it is also true that there are areas wherein the two do not closely overlap, as Blaga himself pointed out in "Schiţa unei autoprezentări filosofice," *Manuscriptum* XVII no. 3 (1986), reprinted in Diaconu and Diaconu, *Dicţionar de Termeni Filosofici ai lui Lucian Blaga* (Bucharest: Univers Enciclopedia, 2000), 12. In particular, there are mystical and intuitive elements in the former that Blaga deems inappropriate to the latter, and a rigorous analyticity in the latter that would be inappropriate to the former.

thinker" in the history of Romanian philosophy.[3] This significant endorsement alerts us to the fact that we have to do here with a thinker whose philosophy will be deep, broad, and creative.[4]

Romania lies at a crossroads of east and west. Its history is shaped by interaction with Greeks and Romans, the Ottoman Empire and the Austrio-Hungarian Empire, industrial Europe and Tsarist and then Soviet Russia. It also experienced waves of invaders, from the Romans and Slavs to Szeklers and Turks. These influences affected Romania in many ways, giving her a Latin tongue with a multilingual vocabulary, traditional rural values with a modern, European system of education, and a respect for cultural diversity coupled with a strong sense of history and national identity. All of this can be seen in Blaga's philosophy – and in his poetry and theater, as well.

Born in a rural village in the interior of the triangle formed by the Carpathian Mountains, Blaga's intellectual development was guided by three main factors: his parents, his schools, and his Transylvanian environs. Blaga's mother, Ana (Moga) Blaga, was the daughter of a Romanian Orthodox priest from an important family in the Romanian Orthodox Church. His father, Isidor Blaga, was the son of a Romanian Orthodox village priest, and although Isidor aspired to higher education, financial exigencies resulted in his appointment to the priesthood vacated at his father's death. Isidor was, however, an avid reader of philosophy, both in Romanian and German. While it can

---

[3] Mircea Eliade, "Rumanian Philosophy," in Paul Edwards, editor in chief, *Encyclopedia of Philosophy* (New York: Macmillan Publishing Co, Inc. and The Free Press, 1967), 233-234.

[4] Also indicative of Blaga's depth is the fact that Blaga was nominated for a Nobel Prize in literature in 1956, and purportedly fell short of receiving the award only due to the machinations of the Communist party.

be supposed that Isidor's example influenced his son in this area, what is known is that the son later borrowed and read the father's books.[5] Thus from his parents Blaga received an orientation towards Romanian Orthodox categories of thought and an interest in philosophy.

Blaga's parents bestowed on him at least one other factor significant to his development as a philosopher: a high estimation of the worth of education. Blaga's parents sacrificed significantly to send their children to private schools, first a private German elementary school in a nearby town, and then a larger, respected high school in a fairly distant city. At the former Blaga acquired proficiency in German, a fact that eventually had great influence on the direction of his philosophy, and received tutelage in the currents of German philosophical and cultural thought. At the latter he studied other languages and advanced his studies of science, philosophy, and religion.[6] He graduated in 1914 with a final thesis on Einstein's relativity and Poincaré's non-Euclidean geometry.[7]

The Transylvania of Blaga's childhood was populated by three major ethnicities: Romanians, Hungarians, and Germans. Blaga's childhood village was a Romanian village, but the nearest town had a significant German population. Blaga benefited from this both because he learned German at an early age and because he learned to see and to value cultural differences. Furthermore, when Blaga determined to pursue higher education, it was the universities in Germany that drew

---

[5] Lucian Blaga, *Hronicul şi cîntecul vîrstelor*, vol. 6, *Opere*, ed. Dorli Blaga (Bucharest: Editura Minerva, 1979), 87.

[6] Blaga's autobiography indicates that he studied Romanian, German, Hungarian, Latin, and Greek. He may also have known Italian and French.

[7] Blaga, *Hronicul şi cîntecul vîrstelor*, 140.

his attention rather than those in Bucharest or France that attracted many of his contemporaries.

Because of the onset of WWI, however, and because of the availability of a scholarship, Blaga ended up taking his undergraduate degree from the Romanian Orthodox seminary in Sibiu, an important Transylvanian city. Although the degree was officially in theology, Blaga's focus was on philosophy. According to his autobiography, his professors were very accommodating of his personal philosophical interests.[8] Upon graduation he enrolled in the PhD program at the University of Vienna, where his studies and his dissertation were in German. The influences of Orthodox theology and German philosophy on Blaga's thinking are both pronounced, the former exemplified by his Platonic and Neo-Platonic elements, his quasi-theistic descriptions of the source of existence, and the nearly apophatic elements of his philosophy of religion, and the latter by his Leibnizian metaphysics, Neo-Kantian epistemology, and Freudian discussions of the subconscious. While the influences of Goethe and Spengler on Blaga's philosophy of culture are obvious, his unique explanation of the source and purpose of culture itself may be at least in part a reflection of his Orthodox background.[9]

---

[8] Blaga, *Hronicul și cîntecul vîrstelor*, 146-151.
[9] Virgil Nemoianu argues that Romanian Orthodoxy is a main channel through which neo-Platonic philosophy influenced the entire "Romanian school of philosophy," including Blaga. Nemoianu, "Mihai Șora and the Traditions of Romanian Philosophy," 594. Furthermore, it seems likely that the mystic and Neo-Platonic elements of Romanian religious culture influenced Blaga's creativity, see Nemoianu, *A Theory of the Secondary* (Baltimore: Johns Hopkins University Press, 1989), 164-166.

Zalmoxis

Blaga's Philosophical System

Blaga's philosophy is described as a "system" because it contains a series of complimentary elements that, when combined, result in a unified whole that philosophically describes and explains all (or nearly all) of the major aspects of human experience. His system includes a metaphysics and cosmology, a detailed and original epistemology, a philosophical anthropology, a philosophy of history, a theory of aesthetics, and a philosophy of religion.[10] Blaga was especially known as a pioneering thinker in the philosophy of culture, which has a prominent place in his system.

Metaphysics

A central feature of Blaga's metaphysics could, with oversimplification, be described as a combination of Plotinus' theory of emanation with Leibnitz' theory of monads. In a Neo-Kantian fashion, he postulates the existence of a hidden, creative force or being who is the source of all else that exists.[11] This "Great Anonymous" or "Anonymous Fund" (Blaga uses the terms interchangeably) created the rest of existence by emanating from itself miniscule immaterial particles ("divine differentials") that combine in a myriad of ways

---

[10] Notably absent from Blaga's system is a system of ethics. Blaga had at one time intended to include a philosophical treatment of ethics, but later decided to deal with ethics via aphorisms rather than philosophical analysis. See Lucian Blaga, *Opere 8: Trilogia cunoașterii*, ed. Dorli Blaga (Bucharest: Editura Minerva, 1983), 58-59. What Blaga's systematic ethics might have been like is discussed by Dan Santa, "Lucian Blaga și universul gnostic" in *Eonul Blaga: Întâiul Veac,* ed. Mircea Borcila (Bucharest: Editura Albatros, 1997), 396-400.

[11] Kant postulates the existence of God as a necessary prerequisite to ethics; Blaga postulates the existence of what he sometimes calls the Anonymous Fund (or Source) as a necessary prerequisite to make sense of the nature of existence as we experience it.

248

toform the building blocks of our world.[12] They are, however, created in such a way that it is impossible for them to ever recombine into a second being equal to the Great Anonymous. In this way the source of everything else perpetuates its own hegemony and assures the preservation of the order of existence.

In addition to this differentiated creation, Blaga suggests a second way that the Great Anonymous preserves cosmic equilibrium: "transcendent censorship."[13] While many metaphysicians have struggled with the question "what is the nature of existence?," and many epistemologists have struggled with "what are the methods of knowledge?," relatively few have sought to answer the question "what is it that impedes our answering of these fundamental questions?" Yet the realization of the magnitude of the difficulty of these questions is one of the key insights of postmodernity, and therefore the question of the nature of this philosophical barrier must be addressed.[14] Blaga takes up this issue, and suggests an answer that is both surprising and philosophically fruitful.

Blaga proposes that this type of ultimate question is difficult to answer, and in some sense unanswerable, because in addition to the ontological limit imposed by the Great Anonymous upon creation

---

[12] This cosmology is discussed in greatest detail in the following books: Lucian Blaga, *Cunoașterea luciferică* (Sibiu, Romania: Tiparul Institutului de arte grafice "Dacia Traiană," 1933), *Cenzura transcendentă. Încercarea metafizică* (Bucharest, Cartea Românească, 1934), and *Diferenţialele divine* (Bucharest: Fundaţia pentru literatură şi artă "Regele Carol II," 1940).

[13] Vasile Băncilă argues that transcendent censorship is the backbone of Blaga's metaphysics (Băncilă, *Lucian Blaga: energie românească,*52).

[14] That Blaga significantly anticipated certain aspects of Postmodernism has been argued by the Romanian philosopher Angela Botez in "The Postmodern Antirepresentationalism (Polanyi, Blaga, Rorty)," *Revue Roumaine de Philosophie et Logique* 41 (1997): 59-70.

(through the means of differentiated creation) the Great Anonymous has also imposed a cognitive limit on creation. He calls this limit "transcendent censorship" because it was initiated beyond the human "spatio-temporal horizon."[15] It was instituted from the very beginning of creation, and is now an inherent aspect of the cosmos, affecting all modes of cognition.[16] It is accomplished via a network of factors, including

obligatory epistemic reliance on the concrete,[17] the intervention of a variety of cognitive structures (including the categories of the understanding[18] and cultural style[19]), the resulting "dissimulation of

---

[15] Blaga, *Cenzura transcendentă,* 451. See also Blaga, *Cunoașterea luciferică,* 404.

[16] Blaga, *Cenzura transcendentă,* 453. Transcendent censorship was enacted in the pre-cosmic stage of genesis, and is not now accomplished through direct intervention, nor is it repeated. Its results also affect animals insofar as animals are capable of cognition. Blaga, *Diferențialele divine,* 184-185.

[17] Blaga, *Cenzura transcendentă,* 456.

[18] In distinction from Kant, Blaga says that the categories of the understanding are subjective, and that their number is not fixed. This is one of the central theses of his PhD dissertation, and is also found in Blaga, *Cenzura transcendentă,* 511, and in greater detail in the sub-chapter "The categorical concepts – subjective or objective" in Lucian Blaga, *Știință și creație* (Sibiu, Romania: Editura "Dacia Traiană," 1942).

[19] Blaga uses the term "stylistic brakes" [frânele stilistice] to indicate the limiting effect of culture on human cognition. While culture is appreciated by humans as a thing of value (and indeed, may well be appreciated by the Great Anonymous as an aspect of creation and human creativity), it is also a limiting factor in human cognition, since all cognition takes place within a cultural milieu and is culturally conditioned. According to Blaga, a result of the stylistic brakes is that human interpretations of the world are as much an expression of style as they are mirrors of objective reality, see Blaga, *Știință și creație,* 160-161.

the transcendent,"[20] and "the illusion of adequacy."[21] Transcendent censorship not only prevents humans from having positive-adequate knowledge of existential mysteries; it prevents them from having "positive-adequate" knowledge of any object of cognition whatsoever. Furthermore, the reader may notice that in contrast to Kantian epistemology, wherein existence is passive in the cognitive event, according to Blaga's theory, existence is active in preventing itself from being known.[22]

According to Blaga, the result of transcendent censorship is that all human knowledge is either dissimulation[23] (in which objects of cognition are represented as being other than they really are), or negative cognition[24] (in which antinomian elements of a cognitive problem are reconciled through the employment of a heuristic "theory idea," which leads to a deepened understanding of the problem without resulting in its complete elimination), or a combination of these.[25] This does not indicate that Blaga is a skeptic: in fact, Blaga rejects skepticism as being too simplistic. He allows that both

---

[20] The dissimulation of the transcendent is the cognizing of reality as other than it actually is, and happens in cognition as a matter of course, Blaga, *Cenzura transcendentă*, 468.

[21] The illusion of adequacy is the mistaken belief on the part of humans that our cognition accurately grasps objects in their essence, Blaga, *Cenzura transcendentă*, 450ff; 488-9. These are also discussed in the chapter "Fenomene, cunoasteri, cordoane cenzoriale" in Lucian Blaga, *Fiinţa istorică* (Cluj-Napoca, Romania: Editura Dacia, 1977).

[22] Blaga, *Cenzura transcendentă*, 452, 456-9.

[23] Blaga, *Cenzura transcendentă*, ch. 3. Blaga also calls this "quasi-cognition."

[24] Blaga, *Cenzura transcendentă*, chapter 5. Blaga also calls this "luciferic cognition."

[25] Blaga, *Cenzura transcendentă*, 516ff.

subjectivism and objectivism have strengths and weaknesses,[26] argues that all cognition is subjective, and explains how cognition succeeds in spite of its subjective elements.[27] Even the "mysteries" of existence are *approachable*, although not ultimately *reachable*, through the strategy which Blaga names "luciferic cognition."[28]

Human existence is characterized by two modes of existence, the "paradisaic" mode, which is the normal state of life in the world, and the "luciferic" mode, which is life lived in the presence of mystery and for the purpose of "revealing" (grappling with, trying to understand) mystery.[29] "Mystery" is a result of the protective limits imposed on creation by the Great Anonymous (transcendent censorship and the discontinuity between creator and creation). Through these means the Great Anonymous gives to humanity its destiny and its purpose in life: its purpose is to create, its destiny is to strive (through creating) to reveal the mysteries of existence. Through this artifice humanity receives a goal, a purpose, and the unique historicity that makes humanity so culturally rich.[30]

---

[26] Blaga, *Cenzura transcendentă,* 507-508.

[27] Blaga, *Cenzura transcendentă,* 512.

[28] Blaga, *Cenzura transcendentă,* 502.

[29] Blaga, *Ființa istorică,* 491-2. This results in an "ontological mutation," a transformation from being a mere living organism ("the paradisaic human") to being an organism that lives "in the horizon of mystery," with the awareness of mystery, ever provoked by this awareness to reach beyond itself, to transcend its inherent limits, and to strive to fathom the depths of the unknown. This transforms humanity into a race of beings that create culture, and sets them apart from other living beings. See Diaconu and Diaconu, *Dictionar de Termeni Filosofici ai lui Lucian Blaga,* 209-211.

[30] Blaga, *Ființa istorică,* 503.

Humanity was created to create. In Blaga's vision, creation is the highest moral virtue, one that is shared by the Great Anonymous and humanity. Humans were created with a creative pattern in their souls so that they would participate in and perpetuate the creative work of the Great Anonymous. Therefore individual cognition, so far from being secularized as some suggest, turns out to be

intimately involved with the transcendent, and that not in spite of its relativity, but exactly because of it.[31] The Great Anonymous designed individual cognition, with its abilities and limits, and designed it in such a way as to maximize the advantages for both humanity and all of existence. Human cognition continually brushes up against the transcendent, fails to conquer it, but is drawn to explore it, to "reveal" it, creatively.

Epistemology

Blaga's epistemology is very detailed, so this summary will relate merely the most salient highlights. Parallel to Blaga's metaphysical distinction between these two modes of human existence is an epistemological distinction between paradisaic and luciferic cognition.[32] Paradisaic cognition is the most common type of "understanding cognition," and represents what is often taken to be the normal approach to knowledge acquisition. Its goal is the

---

[31] Blaga, *Cenzura transcendentă*, 543.

[32] Blaga, *Cenzura transcendentă*, 459. The terms "paradisaic" and "luciferic" are found in Blaga's earlier writing, while in his later writing he switched to "type I" and "type II" cognition, which, while less suggestive, are also less controversial. Paradisaic cognition works within the cognitive boundaries established by the Creator, while luciferic cognition attempts to overcome these boundaries through the reconciliation of the antinomies that often stymie paradisaic cognition.

quantitative or numerical reduction of the mysteries of existence by adding new facts to human knowledge. Paradisaic cognition operates through the application of Neo-Kantian categories of understanding to raw unconceptualized data. It views the objects of cognition as "given," as passive in the cognitive process, being given to the subject through intuition, abstraction, and imagination.[33] Paradisaic cognition is a function of what Blaga calls the "enstatic intellect," which is the human intellect in its ordinary mode of operation.[34] In this mode, the intellect seeks knowledge without attempting to transcend logic.

If paradisaic cognition is the normal mode of understanding, luciferic cognition is the abnormal, the exceptional mode. Luciferic cognition is a method of deepening the understanding of phenomena that involve antinomies.[35] It operates through attempting to resolve paradoxes that arise in paradisaic cognition.[36] It views the paradisaic object as a sign of the mystery that is the actual object. This mystery is partly revealed and partly concealed through paradisaic cognition. When a latent antinomy is discovered in an object, luciferic cognition approaches the antinomy with the tools of negative cognition, attempting to lessen the unknown elements of the mystery (this is called "attenuation of the mystery"). Sometimes an unexpected result is achieved: the mystery is determined to be impenetrable ("permanentization of the mystery"), or more rarely, the mystery is

---

[33] Blaga, *Cunoașterea luciferică*, 315.
[34] Blaga, *Cunoașterea luciferică*, 315-6, 434, 459ff.
[35] A helpful article on the important place of antinomies in Blaga's epistemology is Stephan Afloroaei, "Antinomii ale intelectului ecstatic" in Dumitru Ghișe, Angela Botez, and Victor Botez, *Lucian Blaga – cunoaștere și creație* (Bucharest: Cartea Românească, 1987).
[36] Blaga, *Cunoașterea luciferică*, 349.

found to be even more mysterious than previously understood ("intensification of the mystery").[37]

Luciferic cognition is a function of what Blaga calls the "ecstatic intellect," which is the human intellect in its most intense mode of operation.[38] In this mode, the intellect seeks a fuller understanding of the cognitive object by investigating the aspects of the object that seem to transcend logic. Thus luciferic cognition is the mode of cognition wherein the most difficult problems of understanding are addressed. Concomitantly it and its subdivisions are one of the most interesting insights of Blaga's epistemology.[39] Whereas paradisaic cognition views objects of cognition as "given" to the senses (or intuitions), luciferic cognition views them as partly given, but also partly *hidden*.[40] Paradisaic cognition is subject to the "illusion of adequacy" - the mistaken belief that the object is as it is perceived to be, or more precisely, the mistaken belief that paradisaic cognition is able to grasp the object as it really is. Luciferic cognition begins with the dashing of this illusion.[41] It provokes an internal crisis in an object, and deepens the understanding of the object by probing possible

---

[37] Blaga, *Cunoașterea luciferică,* 325, 434.

[38] The term "ecstatic" is not intended to have any connotation of ecstasy as found in Neo-Platonic mystical union. "Ecstatic" refers to the state (hence "-static") wherein the intellect functions outside (hence "ec-") of its norm.

[39] To read more on luciferic cognition, see Jones, *The Metaphysics of Religion,* 105-17.

[40] Blaga, *Cunoașterea luciferică,* 316. "Given," in this context, implies that the senses are passive in receiving the cognitive content, as in Locke's "simple ideas" resulting directly from experience without any mental in intervention. As has already been noted, according to Blaga's proposed metaphysic, objects of cognition *are* partly hidden, by the Great Anonymous, and for very specific reasons. The distinction between the object of paradisaic cognition and the object of luciferic cognition bears a resemblance to Kant's phenomena-noumena distinction, but has several important differences that Blaga discusses in *Cunoașterea luciferică* (320-2).

[41] Blaga, *Cenzura transcendentă,* 489-491.

problems associated with the object.[42] An investigation that stops at the mere defining of an object as it is "given" overlooks a potentially large number of other facets of knowledge about the object. The benefit of luciferic cognition is that it goes beyond this stopping point of paradisaic cognition.

The question of whether it is better to adhere strictly to logic and therefore reject some part of the empirical data, or to abandon logic and embrace an antinomy, is not easily resolved. Blaga concedes that the separation of intellect and belief would amount to the "suicide of philosophy."[43] Therefore the philosopher must exhaust every possible means of reconciling an antinomy and reserve the method of minus-cognition as a last resort.[44] But Blaga argues that, in order to be true to experience, the intellect must be open to the possibility of breaking from the strictures of logic when necessary. And the only mode of cognition that is capable, to some small degree, of stepping out of its logic-oriented self and reaching beyond itself to something external is luciferic cognition.

Blaga writes that the distinction between paradisaic and luciferic cognition is almost but not quite captured by translating them as "descriptive cognition" and "explanatory cognition." Neither is more empirical than the other.[45] And he concludes that epistemology that

---

[42] Blaga, *Cunoașterea luciferică*, 319.
[43] Lucian Blaga, *Eonul dogmatic* (Bucharest: Cartea Românească, 1931), 262.
[44] Blaga, *Eonul dogmatic*, 272.
[45] Blaga, *Cunoașterea luciferică*, 434.

fails to take into account the important difference between paradisaic and luciferic cognition will necessarily result in confusion.[46]

Philosophy of Culture

Elements of Blaga's metaphysics and epistemology, most notable his theory of human creative destiny, the accompanying doctrines of dissimulated creation and transcendent censorship, and his epistemological constructivism, hint strongly at the significant role that culture plays in Blaga's philosophy. According to Blaga, culture is an inevitable result of the human attempt to reveal/depict/grasp the mysteries of human existence.

Many Romanian commentators have interpreted culture as holding the central place in Blaga's system. According to Blaga, culture is the *sine qua non* of humanness.[47] It is culture more than anything else that distinguishes humanity from other forms of animal life.[48] Likewise, it is culture that distinguishes historical events from all other events that occur in time and space.[49]

According to Blaga's analysis, every cultural creation involves three essential elements: concrete material, metaphorical expression, and style (analyzable into a matrix of elements). The concrete materials of a culture are the physical, intellectual, or spiritual materials that humans utilize in their creations. These are used metaphorically to express ideas, emotions, or intuitions that transcend the material itself.

---

[46] Blaga, *Cunoaşterea luciferică*, 308. Blaga asserts that his explication of the rationalizing of experience in paradisaic and luciferic cognition distinguishes his own epistemology from all other epistemologies, Blaga, *Cunoaşterea luciferică*, 364.

[47] Blaga, *Fiinţa istorică*, 292.

[48] Blaga, *Fiinţa istorică*, 498.

[49] Blaga, *Fiinţa istorică*, 371, 497.

And the particular way that the concrete is metaphorically used reflects the style of the user, which is the product of a number of factors called the "stylistic matrix."

A very important aspect of Blaga's philosophy of culture is his analysis of the categories of the mind and how these categories relate to culture. Although the Kantian influence on this area of Blaga's thought is unmistakable, Blaga adds significantly to Kant's understanding of the categories.[50] According to Blaga, humans are equipped with not one but two sets of intellectual categories. The first of these he names "the categories of the understanding." These categories correspond fairly closely to the Kantian categories. Their role is the organization of sensory data in paradisaic cognition.[51]

Contrary to many scientists, who take categories such as time and space to be objective realities, Blaga agrees with Kant that the categories of the understanding are subjective. Kant's reason for drawing this conclusion is that the conceptual contents of the categories surpass the contents of experiential data, and therefore cannot themselves be a product of experience, and thus must have their source in the mind itself. Blaga writes that the climate (influenced by the Enlightenment and the growing influence of natural science) within which Kant worked prevented him from positing a supernatural source of the categories, and therefore Kant concluded that if they are

---

[50] See especially Blaga, *Ştiinţă şi creaţie* chapters 18 ("Cîteva probleme de teoria cunoaşterii" [Some problems of the theory of knowledge]) and 19 ("Doua tipuri de cunoaştere" [Two types of cognition]).

[51] Blaga, *Ştiinţă şi creaţie*, 176; Lucian Blaga, *Geneza metaforei şi sensul culturii* in *Opere 9: Trilogia Culturii*, ed. Dorli Blaga (Bucharest: Editura Minerva, 1985), 407.

a product of the mind, then they must be subjective.[52] Nonetheless, the conclusion that subjectivity is the only alternative left after the elimination of the possibility of an experiential origin of the categories is mistaken. Blaga points out that there is another option: the categories could be the product of a supernatural source that created them as objective.

In Blaga's view, the categories are in fact the result of a supernatural source, the postulated Great Anonymous who created the cosmos.[53] However, Blaga is in agreement with Kant that the categories are subjective. Blaga's reason for this interpretation of the categories is quite different from Kant's, and has to do with the structure and purpose of cognition. Blaga's reason for believing the categories to be subjective is that, according to his proposed metaphysics, in order to further its purposes in creation, the Great Anonymous does not permit humans to have objective ("positive-adequate") cognition. The categories are one of the means utilized to prevent this. They act as both facilitators and limits to cognition, enabling subjective knowledge but preventing objective knowledge.[54]

According to Kant, the categories of the understanding are a fixed set that is necessarily possessed by all people. In other words, all people have the same immutable categories of the understanding. In reflecting on this, Blaga observes that, while the perception of space, time, and so on appears to be universal, space and time are also

---

[52] Blaga, Știință și creație, 184–85.
[53] Blaga's postulation of the existence of a creator of the universe is discussed in chapter 4: "Blaga's Metaphysics," in Jones, The Metaphysics of Religion.
[54] Blaga, Știință și creație, 185–86.

259

understood in different ways in different cultures.[55] The categories of the understanding, though subjective, are not affected by culture (and do not bear the imprint of style) because they are not human creations—they are created by the Great Anonymous.[56] He accounts for the apparent variability of the categories by proposing that humans have two sets of categories, not one: the cognitive categories of the conscious and the "abyssal" (deep) categories of the subconscious (also called the "stylistic categories").[57] The former are invariable, but the latter are quite variable. Space and time are universal concrete horizons of the conscious. However, their "texture" is determined by the abyssal categories of each individual's subconscious, and is therefore variable. For example, space can be conceived as being tridimensional, flat, undulatory, arched, or other ways.[58] Based on its particular set of abyssal categories, the human subconscious attributes to space and time details of structure that are similar to but more

---

[55] Lucian Blaga, *Orizont și stil* (Bucharest: Fundația pentru literatură și artă "Regele Carol II," 1935), 137–38.

[56] Blaga, *Geneza metaforei și sensul culturii*, 402; *Știință și creație*, 199, 211.

[57] While the existence of a subconscious within the mind is generally taken for granted today, in Blaga's day it was still a controversial issue. Blaga was a contemporary of Freud and Jung and interacts with their views on the subconscious, see *Orizont ∏i stil*, 97. Vasile Dem. Zamfirescu contrasts Blaga with Freud and Jung in his chapter "Filosofia culturii ∏i psihoanaliz| la Lucian Blaga," in *Dimensiunea Metafizică a Operei lui Lucian Blaga*, ed. Angela Botez and A. Firuț| (Bucharest: Editura Științifică, 1996), 271–75. Regarding the stylistic categories, see Blaga, *Șiință și Creație*, 174–76, and ch. 9 ("Doua tipuri de cunoaștere"); and *Geneza metaforei și sensul culturii*, ch. 5 ("Categoriile abisale").

[58] Blaga, *Geneza metaforei și sensul culturii*, 413.

determined than the indeterminate structures of space and time in the conscious mind.[59]

The abyssal categories form a "stylistic matrix" that lies at the base of all cultural creations.[60] The immense number of combinations of the stylistic categories possible within an individual's stylistic matrix accounts for the plethora of possible and actual cultures.[61] Because of this important role in forming culture, the abyssal categories are constitutive of the substance of humanity, whereas the cognitive categories merely enable the integration of objects to the conscious.[62]

Both the cognitive and the abyssal categories are part of the plan for protecting and enhancing created existence. The cognitive categories are one way that the Great Anonymous implements "transcendent censorship," while the abyssal categories are a means of implementing "transcendent braking."[63] The two types of categories work together to fulfill the Creator's "principle of the conservation of mystery."[64] The stylistic matrix is a set of stylistic categories that determines the results of an individual's creative endeavors.[65] The four

---

[59] Blaga, *Orizont și stil*, 109. In the words of Vasile Muscă, with the introduction of the stylistic categories, "Blaga operates a transfer of criticism from the upper level of the consciousness, the seat of the cognitive activities the analysis of which preoccupied Kant, to the dark basement of the subconscious, the hearth of creative activity." Vasile Muscă, "Specificul creației culturale românești în cîmpul filosofiei," in *Lucian Blaga*, ed. Ghiţe, Botez, and Botez, 469.

[60] Blaga, *Geneza metaforei și sensul culturii*, 409; *Fiinţa istorică*, 498.

[61] Blaga, *Geneza metaforei și sensul culturii,* 412–413.

[62] Blaga, *Orizont și stil*, 133.

[63] "Transcendent censorship" and "transcendent braking" are the strategies by which the Creator prevents the arising of any cognitive rivals in the universe, an occurrence that Blaga indicates would destabilize the universe. Together they serve to thwart positive-adequate cognition on the part of any created being.

[64] Blaga, *Fiinţa istorică*, 490, 502–3; *Ştiinţă și creaţie*, 176 (footnote).

[65] The term "stylistic field" is sometimes used as a synonym for stylistic matrix, as in Blaga, *Fiinţa istorică*, ch. 5, "Campurile stilistice;" see also 420, 485. Liviu

primary components of any stylistic matrix are the horizon of the subconscious, an axiological accent, a particular sense of destiny, and a particular formative aspiration (*nazuinţa formativă*).[66] These, together with an unnumbered quantity of secondary components, make up the stylistic matrix of the subconscious mind. Two different creative styles can be separated by as few as one of these secondary factors.[67] This explains why and how creations within a particular culture bear certain similarities and also why they are not identical.[68] Furthermore, it explains why cultural creations have a sense of fittingness and context. A judgment that a particular creation "lacks style" may be nothing more than an indication that there are subtle differences between the matrices of the creator and the critic.[69]

The stylistic matrix is the inner horizon of the subconscious, and functions according to its own norms, relatively independent of the conscious mind. The stylistic matrix is responsible for the unity of attitudes, emphases, and aspirations that distinguish one culture from another and that give to a person's conscious mind the support of continuity and to a person's subconscious the connection to a

---

Antonesei's chapter "Repere pentru o filosofie a culturii," in *Lucian Blaga*, ed. Ghiţe, Botez, and Botez, 399–411, is a very nice study of the importance of the "stylistic matrix" concept to Blaga's philosophy of culture and the influences of psychoanalysis, morphology, and neo-Kantianism in the development of the concept.

[66] Blaga, *Orizont şi stil*, 152ff., 175, 179; *Geneza metaforei şi sensul culturii*, 410.

[67] Blaga, *Ştiinţă şi creaţie*, 176–78; *Orizont şi stil*, 175. In some places (e.g., *Orizont şi Sstil*, 177) Blaga lists five factors, listing the spatial and temporal horizons of the subconscious separately. In other places he includes the spatial and temporal horizons under the single heading "horizon of the subconscious" (e.g., *Orizont şi stil*, 175). I follow this later practice in my enumeration of four factors.

[68] Blaga, *Orizont şi stil*, 177, 182–83; *Fiinţa istorică*, 420–39.

[69] Blaga, *Orizont şi stil*, 177-8; 184–85. The chapter "Interferenţe stilistice" in *Fiinţa istorică* discusses the different ways that stylistic matrices relate to each other.

collectivity.[70] Furthermore, the existence of stylistic matrices witnesses to the creative destiny given to humanity by the Creator.[71]

Blaga's philosophy of culture and his epistemology are closely integrated. As already pointed out, according to Blaga's analysis, there are two types of cognition: paradisaic and luciferic. The former increases knowledge quantitatively, through the numerical reduction of the mysteries of existence by adding new facts to human knowledge. It utilizes the cognitive categories. The latter increases knowledge qualitatively, through deepening the understanding of the mystery of a cognitive object. This deepening of the understanding involves creative constructs that provide interpretive explanations of the phenomena in question. Since all creative acts are affected by a stylistic matrix, these acts of luciferic cognition are as well. They operate through the application of both the cognitive and the stylistic categories.

Luciferic cognition is limited by transcendent censorship via the cognitive categories. The stylistic categories do not affect paradisaic cognition.[72] Luciferic cognition is limited by both transcendent censorship and the stylistic categories. Therefore all knowledge acquired via luciferic cognition is conditioned by the culture ("style") of the knowing subject.[73] The stylistic categories function both positively and negatively in cognition, and these two functions are intrinsically related. They function as a structural medium for revelation of mystery

---

[70] Blaga, *Orizont și stil*, 186.

[71] Blaga, *Geneza Metaforie și sensul culturii*, 414.

[72] This does not imply that paradisaic cognition is not interpretive—all human knowledge of this world is interpretive, even paradisaic cognition, which interprets based on the cognitive categories. Lucian Blaga, *Experimentul și spiritul matematic* (Bucharest: Editura Științifică, 1969), 657.

[73] Blaga, *Știintă și creație*, 199, 211.

and as a limit to this revelation ("stylistic brakes"). Thus while the abyssal categories lead humans to create, they also prevent human creativity from reaching absolute adequacy.[74]

Corresponding to the two types of cognition and the two types of limits on cognition, there are two definitions of truth that spring from Blaga's philosophy of culture. In luciferic cognition, truth consists in a relation of correspondence between an idea and reality.[75] This is what Blaga names "natural truth." This type of truth involves the application of the cognitive categories to empirical data. Because the cognitive categories are not influenced by culture, "natural truth" is not subject to cultural influences.[76]

What is judged to be true in luciferic cognition, on the other hand, is relative to one's stylistic matrix. What is judged to be true does not depend only upon the criteria of logic and concrete intuition. It involves style, culture, and a feeling of resonance between the proposition and the cognitive subject.[77] As Blaga states, "Judgments of appreciation, which refer to 'constructed' truths, will vary therefore according to how the people's stylistic matrices vary."[78] This is because what is being judged is not simply the relation between an idea and a supposedly observable reality, but the relation between an idea that is a theoretical construct and a reality that is not directly observable. The

---

[74] Blaga, *Fiinţa istorică*, 492–94.

[75] "ecuaţie între idee şi realitate" (in Blaga, *Geneza metaforei şi sensul culturii*, 417). Blaga is well aware that this definition of truth raises a critiriological issue, but we cannot enter into that discussion here.

[76] Blaga, *Geneza metaforei şi sensul culturii*, 417–18. Both types of cognition attempt to reveal mystery. The former does so in a cognitive way that is subject to specific limits, and the latter does so in a cognitive-constructive way that is subject to additional limits, 447, 449ff.

[77] Blaga, *Geneza metaforei şi sensul culturii*, 417–18; see also *Ştiinţă şi creaţie*, 180.

[78] Blaga, *Geneza metaforei şi sensul culturii*, 418.

fact that the reality is not directly observable necessitates the constructive nature of the idea. The constructive nature of the idea implicates the incorporation of culture (since all constructs are cultural constructs according to Blaga's analysis). And the incorporation of culture implicates the employment of the stylistic categories, as much in the appreciation (or at least evaluation) of the idea as in its construction.

That luciferic cognition involves culture in its truth-judgments has implications that reach far beyond philosophy. Science, the humanities, religion – and poetry and theatre as well – are affected by the stylistic categories. Like the cognitive categories, the stylistic categories both facilitate and limit cognition. In this way the two types of categories work together to fulfill the Great Anonymous' "principle of the conservation of mystery."[79]

Blaga's philosophy of culture also dovetails with his metaphysics. Blaga's metaphysical system posits the existence of a single source of all other existents. It also suggests that this source created the cosmos in such a way as to both perpetuate and preserve creation. It created humanity with specific abilities and limits that both

---

[79] Blaga, *Fiinţa istorică*, 490, 502–3; *Ştiinţă si creaţie*, 176 (footnote). This is the principle whereby the Great Anonymous protects and furthers creation through preventing the arising of cognitive rivals that could destabilize the cosmos. It is implemented through the strategies of transcendent censorship and transcendent braking.

motivate and enable humanity to approach mystery, but that also prevent humanity from eliminating mystery.[80]

Blaga's philosophy of culture elaborates one of the devices that the originator of the cosmos put in place to accomplish these goals. That device is culture, understood as a collection of stylistic factors. Culture is key to perpetuating the creator's creative act, for culture is essential to human creativity. Culture is also key to preserving creation, for it prevents humanity from accurately revealing mystery through creative acts, which (according to Blaga) could endanger the cosmos by allowing a cognitive rival to the creator.[81]

The creator, the Great Anonymous, protects itself from the possibility of human rivalry by the stylistic limiting of human revelatory acts. It also prevents this rivalry by creating humanity in such a way that humans put a positive value on style rather than viewing style and culture as limits imposed upon humanity (Blaga calls this tactic "transcendent conversion").[82] According to Blaga's metaphysics, culture is a positive value, since it is the expression of human creativity and genius and an extension of the creativity of the

---

[80] The creator uses the cognitive categories to limit cognition and the stylistic categories to limit construction. When humanity tries to penetrate mystery, it turns to the immediate, but this way is blocked by transcendent censorship. Humanity therefore turns to creative constructs, but that way is blocked by stylistic braking. Therefore humanity never completely succeeds in penetrating mystery. In this way humanity is maintained in its permanently creative state. Blaga, *Geneza metaforei și sensul culturii*, 450–51.

[81] Perhaps this would be a destabilizing situation because a rival might not been in accord with the creator's plan for the cosmos and might attempt to introduce a plan of its own, or perhaps because this situation would result in war between rival supreme beings. Alternatively, it may be that Blaga views this situation as perilous because of the inherent contradiction of the existence of two ultimate beings in one cosmos.

[82] Blaga, *Diferențialele divine*, 179, and Lucian Blaga, *Arta și valoare*, in *Opere 10: Trilogia valorilor*, ed. Dorli Blaga (Bucharest: Editura Minerva, 1987), 631–32.

Great Anonymous itself. At the same time culture is also a necessary and useful limit upon human revelation of the mysterious. The relativity that it imposes upon all human creations has the perhaps tragic effect of isolating humanity from the absolute, but Blaga asserts that at the same time it gives humanity a dignity beyond comparison.[83]

One of the strengths of Blaga's philosophy of culture, and in particular his view on the thwarting of the human aspiration toward the transcendent, is that it confers meaning upon the relativity of all human productions. That human creations are always of finite scope, limited duration, and mitigated success is often viewed as a human shortcoming. Blaga's philosophy of culture provides an explanation for these "shortcomings" that shows their value and removes their condemnation. Humanity's aspiration toward the transcendent is laudable, and the failure to reach this goal is a result of important factors that are necessarily beyond the human reach.[84] The creation of humanity with an insatiable desire for the transcendent is, according to Blaga's philosophy of culture, neither indicative of a shortcoming on the part of humanity, nor an act of maliciousness on the part of the Great Anonymous, but rather is an expression of the care that the

---

[83] Lucian Blaga, *Aspecte antropologice*, in *Opere 11: Trilogia cosmologic/*, ed. Dorli Blaga (Bucharest: Editura Minerva, 1988), 293, *Fiinţa istorică*, 467 ("tragic and wonderful destiny"); *Geneza metaforie şi sensul culturii*, 459.

[84] This philosophy was perhaps of some comfort to Blaga himself, whose struggle to reach God or grasp the ultimate meanings of the universe is reflected in both his poetry and his philosophy, as is explained in Keith Hitchins' introduction to Brenda Walker's translation, *Complete Poetical Works of Lucian Blaga* (Iaşi, Romania; Oxford; and Portland, Oregon: The Center for Romanian Studies, 2001), 45-48.

Great Anonymous has for its creation.[85] It is also responsible for much of what makes humanity special: human creativity and culture.

Resources for Further Study

This brief introduction to Blaga's philosophy has of necessity passed over many significant and interesting areas that would be necessary to a complete philosophical system. Blaga's system treats many other issues, including philosophy of science, philosophy of history, philosophical anthropology, a more completely developed theory of aesthetics, and philosophy of religion. For those who read Romanian, resources for the study of Blaga's philosophy are readily available. Many of his own books of philosophy, numbering about 35 in total if we include books and collections of articles published posthumously, have been republished in recent years. Secondary literature also abounds.

However, to readers who do not know Romanian but would like to learn more about Blaga's philosophy, resources are more scarce. So far only small fragments of Blaga's philosophy have been translated into English. There are, however, a number of articles in English that discuss aspects of Blaga's philosophy. One of the earliest sources is Mircea Eliade's brief discussion of Blaga in his entry on "Rumanian Philosophy" in Macmillan's *Encyclopedia of Philosophy*. Somewhat more detailed is Keith Hitchins' introduction to Brenda Walker's translation of Blaga's poetry.[86] This piece is 26 pages long, and although

---

[85] Blaga, *Geneza metaforie și sensul culturii,* 452.
[86] Keith Hitchins, "Introduction," *Complete Poetical Works of Lucian Blaga,* trans. Brenda Walker, 23-48.

it is not devoted exclusively to Blaga's philosophy, it provides an excellent general introduction to Blaga's thought. Mircea Flonta's entry on Blaga in the *Routledge Encyclopedia of Philosophy On-Line* is more detailed and very accurate.[87]

Virgil Nemoianu has two short but insightful discussions of Blaga's philosophy. The first is contained in the article "Mihai Sora and the Traditions of Romanian Philosophy" in *Review of Metaphysics*.[88] The second is the chapter "The Dialectics of Imperfection" in Nemoianu's book *A Theory of the Secondary*.[89] The Bucharest philosopher Angela Botez has published several articles introducing Blaga's thought and comparing Blaga with better-known philosophers. These articles are "Lucian Blaga and the Complementary Spiritual Paradigm of the 20th Century,"[90] "Comparativist and Valuational Reflections on Blaga's Philosophy,"[91] and "The Postmodern Antirepresentationalism (Polanyi, Blaga, Rorty),"[92] all of which appeared in the journal *Revue Roumaine de Philosophie et Logique*. Her article "Michael Polanyi and Lucian Blaga as Philosophers of Knowledge" is available on line at http://www.bu.edu/wcp/Papers/Comp/ CompBote.htm. Another Romanian academic, Bazil Munteanu, has published an article

---

[87] Mircea Flonta, "Blaga, Lucian." In *Routledge Encyclopedia of Philosophy On-Line*, Taylor & Francis Group, http://www.rep.routledge.com.

[88] Nemoianu, "Mihai Şora and the Traditions of Romanian Philosophy," 591-605.

[89] Nemoianu, *A Theory of the Secondary: Literature, Progress, and Reaction,* 153-170.

[90] Angela Botez, "Lucian Blaga and the Complementary Spiritual Paradigm of the 20th Century," *Revue Roumaine de Philosophie et Logique* 37 (1993): 51-55.

[91] Angela Botez, "Comparativist and Valuational Reflections on Blaga's Philosophy," *Revue Roumaine de philosophie et Logique* 40 (1996): 153-162.

[92] Angela Botez, "The Postmodern Antirepresentationalism (Polanyi, Blaga, Rorty)," *Revue Roumaine de Philosophie et Logique* 41 (1997): 59-70.

introducing Blaga's philosophy in the same journal, "Lucian Blaga, Metaphysician of Mystery and Philosopher of Culture."[93]

There are also a number of web pages devoted to Blaga. The *Wikipedia* entry on Blaga is quite brief (http://en.wikipedia.org/wiki/Lucian_Blaga). The *Answers.com* entry (http://www.answers.com/topic/lucian-blaga) is more detailed, though it misstates that Blaga's fourth philosophical trilogy "remained in the project stage." (Blaga completed this trilogy, but was not able to publish it during his lifetime. It has been published posthumously as *Trilogia cosmologică*.)[94] The British philosopher and editor Richard Allen has several pages on his website devoted to Blaga (http://homepage.ntlworld.com/rt.allen/life.html) and a CD with extracts from Blaga's works. The *Welcome to Romania* and *Simply Romania* web sites also have pages dedicated to Blaga (http://www.ici.ro/romania/culture/l_blaga.html; http://www.simplyromania.com/).

As far as I know, the only book in English entirely devoted to Blaga's philosophy is my own *The Metaphysics of Religion: Lucian Blaga and Contemporary Philosophy*. My article "Culture and Interreligious Understanding According to the Romanian Philosopher Lucian Blaga" will soon appear in the *Journal of Ecumenical Studies*. I am also working on a translation of Blaga's last book of philosophy, *The Historical Being* (Fiinţa istorică).

---

[93] Basile Munteanu, "Lucian Blaga, Metaphysician of Mystery and Philosopher of Culture," *Revue Roumaine de Philosophie et Logique* 39 (1995): 43-46.
[94] Lucian Blaga, *Opere 11: Trilogia Cosmologică*, ed. Dorli Blaga (Bucharest: Editura Minerva, 1988).

Doris C. Plantus

Michael S. Jones, PhD

Liberty University

Zalmoxis

Doris C. Plantus